The Fairy Tale
C O O K B O O K

The Fairy Tale
COOKBOOK

Sandré Moore

Cumberland House Publishing
Nashville, Tennessee

Published by Cumberland House Publishing, Inc., 431 Harding Industrial Drive, Nashville, Tennessee 37211.

Jacket design by Unlikely Suburban Design
Text design by Julie Pitkin

Library of Congress Cataloging-in-Publication Data

Moore, Sandré,
    The fairy tale cookbook : fun recipes for families to create and eat together / Sandré Moore.
        p. cm.
    Includes bibliographical references and index.
    ISBN 1-58182-093-3 (pbk. : alk. paper)
    1. Cookery, American. 2. Fairy tales. I. Title.

  TX715.M8265 2000
  641.5973—dc21

                                                        00-064423

Printed in the United States of America
1 2 3 4 5 6 7 8 — 04 03 02 01 00

For Rich, the greatest chef I know, who has helped me
cook up a life full of delicious times
and for
Tom, a Dad who taught me that failure and determination
were the most important ingredients in success
and for
Alex, Andie, and Ariel, who make me laugh with my mouth full

Contents

The Fairy Tale
COOKBOOK

A Word to Parents

The smell of chicken frying on top of the stove the old-fashioned, greasy way in a cast-iron skillet takes my mind back immediately to my grandmother's kitchen. And if you throw in the strong, full-bodied aroma of coffee percolating, suddenly no matter where I am, I hear the clack-clack-clack of a hand-cranked ice cream freezer, the hum of an extra refrigerator out in her garage, always stocked with ice-cold Coca-Colas, the laughter and gabbing of grown-ups sharing stories, like where they were when they heard that Pearl Harbor had been bombed. I see the happy phantoms of sticky, grinning cousins sitting on the back steps eating watermelon while wiggling bare toes in sweet, cool grass. My memory calls up White Shoulders perfume hanging on the sleepy-hot summer air and there she is, in all her crinkly-petticoated, full-skirted glory, my grandmother, Maggie, clucking and scolding and fussing around her almost painfully bright white-tiled kitchen in Tyler, Texas, smacking sneaky fingers around her cutting board and kissing cheeks of siblings, children, and grandchildren.

Even now, as a supposed grown-up, when I experience certain smells from kitchens or markets, I'm six or seven again instantly. It's Christmas every time I smell vanilla, because that will always be the signal for the beginning of the pre-holiday chocolate chip cookie ritual. Snuggled down inside my blankets, trying to hang onto the last five minutes of sleep I'll get before starting a hectic day, the unmistakable aroma of bacon frying in the kitchen will drift through the bedroom door, and though I live in a seaport in a semitropical climate now, my mind tells me that if I hurry over to my bedroom window I might catch the breathtaking sight of the undisturbed crust of blue-white snow that fell overnight on my backyard in Denver when I was twelve. Shellfish always brings back my eighteenth birthday dinner with my dad in a little restaurant on Fisherman's Wharf in San Francisco and the first time I knew I was becoming an adult because my father treated me as an equal. In a slightly bizarre cross-cultural reference, the exotic Eastern perfume of curry never brings to mind Indian cuisine, but the best Indonesian meal of my life thus far with my dad and my brother, served on starchy-white table linens from whimsically shaped serving dishes in a restaurant in the middle of the friendly, bustling city of Amsterdam.

What do foods make you remember?

Somehow, as a mother myself, I couldn't deal with the idea that my children would smile dreamily and fondly remember their special childhood moments whenever someone opened a can of Beef-a-Roni.

My husband and I love to spend time in the kitchen and have tried very hard to set aside time to share not only our love of cooking, but a sense of being a family with our children by involving them in the preparation, cooking and sharing of food.

So many parents I've talked to lately sigh deeply and lament that they must now decorate their homes around their television sets. The family room or den has become the hub of family activities. How many times has any parent thought to him or herself, "Why don't my kids ever pay attention or listen to me the first time I tell them something?" The answer is they probably can't hear you over the volume of the video game or the latest cartoon trend.

Don't you hate it when our parents and grandparents are right? The heart of the home is the kitchen. Just as you monitor the amount of bad cholesterol you consume, watch the fat intake in your diet and exercise moderately to keep your heart healthy, try doing some preventive maintenance on your family by seeing to it that your home's heart is healthy too. Dad, teach the youngest one to play checkers at the kitchen table while you're waiting for that important phone call. Mom, you'd be surprised how many heart-to-heart talks start with sharing the preparation of a lasagne. Don't get me wrong; I'm not preaching, just speaking from experience and trial and error. We used to have a small television in our kitchen, too. We got rid of it. Now, we play word games while we eat and even my cynical darling teens don't want to leave the table because they're having too much fun with the family.

Never thought you'd hear that phrase, did you? Me neither.

It doesn't happen overnight, and it doesn't happen all at once. It's a gradual process of making your time together as a family important and enjoyable. But I'll tell you why my husband and I have done our best to make it happen—I look at my youngest daughter today and think to myself, "Today, she is exactly eight years and two days old. She will never be exactly that age again. If I lose this day because I'm too busy or tired, I will never get it back again. And someday, when she's off at college or Corporate Vice President in Charge of Widgets for a multinational corporation halfway around the world, all I will be able to think is, 'I wish I had that day back.'"

There is one more perk for parents that I included in this book. It contains a couple of tried and true and extremely sneaky ways to get little kids to eat some foods they would not normally stay in the same house with. I'm sure, once you catch on to the method of my madness, you will come up with your own tricks of the parenting trade. Let me know; I'm sure grandchildren are inevitable, given the circumstances.

Kids in the Kitchen
COOKING SAFETY

Two vivid and warm memories of my childhood are sitting on a kitchen chair or stool while my parents bustled and laughed around the kitchen, and grown-ups in my life reading me everything from the Sunday comics to bedtime fairytales. Both gave me a feeling of security and family. Families come in all shapes and sizes these days and I think the variety is wonderful. So, no matter how large or how small your family is, I hope your family will have fun with this book.

The first thing we need to talk about is safety in the kitchen. Cooking dinner together loses something if it's punctuated by a visit to the emergency room. Kids and parents need to follow basic kitchen safety rules:

1. Tie back long hair, away from your face.
2. Grown-ups handle sharp tools (knives, for example) and all jobs using these tools.
3. Handles on pots and pans should be turned so they don't stick out over the edge of the stove where they might tempt short people to grab them.
4. Handle everything hot with pot holders, preferably one for each hand.
5. If you have a gas stove, keep everything away from the burners—fingers, hair, pot holders, towels, paper, small pieces of food, etc.
6. Talk about what to do if there is a fire in the kitchen and the different types of fires. If possible, keep a small, charged fire extinguisher in the kitchen.
7. Do not reach across a hot burner or boiling pot to stir or pick up something else on the stove.
8. We're cooking together, so do not leave children in the kitchen alone for any reason. Kids, do not leave parents alone in the kitchen (they sneak bites!)

9. Everyone who is cooking must *listen and follow instructions*. Because there are a lot of potentially dangerous things in a kitchen, anyone who doesn't listen to instructions has to leave.

10. Everyone stands or sits on something non-wobbly and everyone gives every-one else enough room to work. No crowding, no push-ing, and ABSOLUTELY NO ARGUING. Anyone disobeying Rule #10 will be eaten.

11. Parents know who is the right age to do which job. Make sure *everyone* participates safely.

12. Everyone shares clean-up duties.

13. For health safety, wash hands. Wash hands. Wash hands. Contrary to popular kid belief, these is no actual legal limit on the number of times you can wash your hands in one day.

Each recipe in this book has K and P designations in it.

K is a job that is probably good for kids to do;

P is a parent job. Your family can read the recipe and decide who should do which job.

COOK SAFELY!

Make It Easy On Yourself
THE RIGHT TOOLS FOR THE JOB

I tried to bluff my way through cooking for years, using this pan as a substitute for that one and owning only one real kitchen knife which I attempted to use for everything. If I had known how much time, money and wasted, ruined food I could have saved myself by simply investing in the kitchen utensils actually called for in recipes or suggested by professional chefs, the frugal part of me would have made a bee-line for the first store that sold cooking paraphernalia.

You don't have to invest in expensive cookware sets; keep it simple. And I don't think it's necessary to buy every kitchen gadget on the market. My father, the acknowledged "King of Gadgets," once bought an electric hot dog cooker. He inserted hot dogs onto the spikes on either side of the machine, then turned on the power. It cooked the hot dogs by passing an electrical current from one metal spike, through the hot dog, to the other metal spike, theoretically. In other words, it electrocuted hot dogs. Which, if I remember correctly, is pretty much how they tasted. My little brother and I referred to the contraption as "Frankenweenie." Dad finally got rid of the thing one day when it blew up three hot dogs in a shower of sparks.

Here are a few of the items your kitchen should have:

A good measuring cup—the ones I like best are glass and hold as much as 4 cups, but you can always get by with a set of cups of varying sizes (for example: ¼ cup, ⅓ cup, ½ cup, 1 cup).

Measuring spoons—the most common (and inexpensive) are aluminum, and the spoons, in various sizes you'll need, are held together on a ring. The only real requirement is accuracy, so I suggest a set with ⅛ teaspoon, ¼ teaspoon, ½ teaspoon, 1 teaspoon, and 1 tablespoon. Don't use the spoons out of your silverware drawer; you'll never get the measurements right.

Baking sheet—also called a cookie sheet. I like the ones that have a slightly raised lip around the rim. Some types are non-stick and some need to be greased to keep things from sticking.

Skillet—a large, flat pan with shallow, raised sides. The one I use the most is cast iron, but they come in many different materials. I also have a flat cast iron griddle, but if you don't have or can't find a griddle, you can use a skillet instead.

Saucepans—pans with deeper sides in various sizes. The biggest ones can be used to cook stews and soups, the smaller ones are good for melting and combining ingredients.

Cutting board—a good cutting board can be made of acrylic, wood or marble, is about 12 x 20 inches and can be used for cutting, rolling dough, kneading bread, and basically, for a workspace. We have four wooden cutting boards of different sizes so everyone can work at the same time. Be sure to clean your board thoroughly every time you use it.

Stirring spoons—when children are helping in the kitchen, I find it handy to have long-handled wooden spoons. They don't conduct heat like metal spoons and keep smaller fingers away from hot pans.

Knives—the brand name or type of metal of a knife isn't nearly as important as the sharpness of the edge and the size. The main rule to remember with knives is use the right size for the job. A small, sharp knife for paring, a large knife for cutting vegetables, etc., and a keen, easy-to-handle knife for trimming meat, poultry, etc.

Pot holders—can be made of many materials and are good to have in large supply. I prefer the solid, well-padded cotton pot holders that are washable to the knitted or ornamental ones. Oven mittens are also a good idea if you have them.

Pie pans, cake pans, casseroles — we have collected a huge assortment of ovenware over the years and believe me, dishes just come out better when baked in the appropriate pans. You can experiment with casseroles of different sizes, materials and shapes, but try not to overload them (it's also a good idea to put a baking sheet underneath them in the oven to catch any drips). I also learned the hard way that when a recipe says '9-inch cake pan' that's what it means. Every time I'm tempted to fudge on the size of a cake pan, I remember the interesting chocolate soup that resulted from a brownie recipe baked in the wrong size and shape pan.

Stove — can be either gas or electric. Gas heat is easier to regulate because you can see the flame, but is more dangerous for young chefs for the same reason. Please note that HIGH is a setting seldom used because it doesn't cook food faster, just hotter.

Oven — one way to make sure your oven heats food evenly is by putting plain, unglazed terra cotta tiles on the bottom rack. Every oven heats a little differently, so you might want to use an oven thermometer on the middle rack to test how accurate the temperature setting is

Bowls — small bowls are great for preparing measured ingredients before you begin to cook. You'll also need mixing bowls for combining ingredients, and this is another case of "the more the merrier." If you have lots of good-sized mixing bowls everyone can help in their own work space.

Optional or Occasional Tools:

Electric mixer — Please watch little fingers that are so curious around those metal beaters. You don't necessarily need an electric mixer; you can always beat batter by hand with a spoon. An electric mixer saves a little time and energy.

Whisk or eggbeater—another time-saver. There are recipes that benefit from the "lighter touch" you get from a whisk rather than an electric mixer.

Peeler—my choice for a kid tool so they can help peel vegetables with less danger to fingers

Plastic "picnic" knives—another great kid tool. Use these to cut softer foods like banana slices or hot dog bites.

Shopping for Ingredients
Oh, the Foods We Will See!

Grocery shoppers usually fall into two broad categories: people who like to "get it over with" as quickly as possible because they think of shopping as one more chore on a long list of things to do; people who have learned to "stop and smell the cantaloupes" (because that's the best test for ripeness) and revel in spending hours cruising through their local supermarket, mercado or farmer's market. Then, of course, there are "combination shoppers," people who are sometimes rushed and shop alone, but take the whole family on a grocery run when time permits. Here are some family shopping tips for each type:

TIME CRUNCH SHOPPERS

If scheduling time together is something that has to be managed carefully, by all means keep the shopping quick and easy so you can spend your "quality time" cooking together. For this kind of shopping, make a list of ingredients you'll need the evening before you go shopping. Stick to your list and go by yourself to a supermarket you're familiar with. All these will save you time and money.

FAMILY "GROCERIES AND GAMES" SHOPPERS

Sit down with older children and make a list of ingredients to shop for, along with other things you might need. Every age group can have fun grocery shopping -- small shoppers can tell you the names of colors you point to, school-age kids can use aisle numbers to count, everyone can learn the names of fruits and vegetables. Pre-teens can tell you the best unit price on different brands of the same item by doing the math. Everyone can learn the four basic food groups by identifying them in the grocery cart, and everyone can help count the number of items and help you decide whether or not you can get in the Express Line or not. A word to the wise: everyone eats before you go shopping, schedule the trip at a time when pint-sized assistants will not be cranky, and whatever the length of your normal shopping trip—double it. Answering questions takes time.

FAMILY SPEED SHOPPING

This is a combination of limited time and needing or wanting to take the whole family with you. A parent makes the list and explains before you get out of the car that speed is the name of the game. The rules for the game are: 1. Everyone stays together, 2. Everyone helps locate the items, 3. Nobody wastes time arguing. Check a watch or clock and tell everyone the time you want to be finished shopping. Ready, set, SHOP!

OTHER VARIATIONS

If you have children who are 5th graders or older, divide up the grocery list and have them gather their items in a separate shopping cart and meet you at an agreed upon location in the store.

Have older children bring a calculator with them and keep a running total. Next trip, have them estimate whether you will spend less, the same or more. Everyone can look through the grocery ads or coupon supplements in the newspaper and identify items your family buys or foods they particularly like. Have them cut out coupons or tell you which stores have the best prices.Shopping for ingredients can be a great opportunity to teach children budgeting time and money, how to identify freshness in foods, talk about nutrition, and learning and practicing good "public place" manners. Remember that recipes taste best when you have the right ingredients, but that doesn't necessarily mean the most expensive foods.

Big, Beautiful, Bountiful Breakfasts

Once upon a time, there was a nice family, who, like families everywhere, ate about two or three meals a day. The adults in the family worked hard, inside and outside of their home, the children had busy schedules, too, and everybody in the family thought that meals were a kind of necessary evil.

The parents in the family thought of shopping for food and taking time to cook it as a chore. The children in the family thought that being forced to sit in front of a plate of food at certain times of the day was a stupid waste of kid time and that consuming food was a hated duty. The parents also felt guilty about the foods they sometimes served because they thought growing children would somehow shrivel and die if they weren't given a vegetable or fruit with every meal.

If mornings at your house are anything like our house, there have been days when, no matter what your good intentions, your preteen couldn't eat through her tears because her bathing suit for first period swim team practice has suddenly disappeared and Coach is going to yell at her and make her run 500 laps, your eldest has a new friend who convinced her that pigs are the noblest creatures on Earth and that anyone who consumes bacon or ham is one step away from being a cannibal, and your youngest, who was completely ready to walk out the front door five minutes ago, is now strolling into the kitchen au naturel carrying his disposable diaper in his hand, and your mate is doing that morning thing where he or she stands at the end of the counter, seemingly unconcerned that the ants are escaping from your child's science project, finishing a cup of coffee and checking his or her watch every three minutes and clearing his or her throat.

The horror, the horror...

It is my own considered opinion that, if breakfast is the most important meal of the day, the only requirement is that they eat something. Rosettes made from apples, Anglo-Saxon wheat pancakes cooked in an authentic Celtic hearth, or Eggs Benedict are wonderful, but let's live in the real world for a moment, shall we?

For busy work days and school days, I personally don't think there's anything wrong with convenience foods like breakfast bars or toaster pop-ups if they're supplemented with a couple of cantaloupe cubes or watermelon or even cheese bites, and those can be prepared the night before and refrigerated.

When I lived at home with my parents, my younger brother went through a period of time when he would only eat Veal Parmesan and cooked spinach for breakfast. We found cooking bags and convenience foods that let him have what he wanted with a preparation time of only 10 minutes.

The reasonable (and fun thing) to do is to prepare big or time-consuming meals when everyone can enjoy them. Make Saturday lunch a family event or make Sunday brunch the time you'll all cook and sit down together to eat and revel in the good and nutritious foods you've all put together.

With that in mind, here are some big, beautiful, bountiful Breakfasts....

KING BABAR'S FRENCH TOAST
(with Peanut Butter
and Honey Topping)
FIT FOR AN ELEPHANT

What do you say when you find an elephant in pajamas in the kitchen?
You say, "Good morning, Your Majesty," if the pachyderm in question is the
noble Babar. Being a king can really keep a dad busy, even when he's an
elephant. King Babar, the elephant, thinks that relaxing and making time
for his family, including the lovely Queen Celeste, the children, and even
the Old Lady, who is like a member of the family, is very important. That's
why on Sunday mornings, Babar and his family hang out in the palace
kitchen in their jammies and he makes everyone his famous French Toast.
Queen Celeste enjoys hers topped with powered sugar, but the children,
especially Alexander and Isabelle, love Babar's famous peanut butter and
honey topping. You might like it, too, even if you are not an elephant.
After they eat, everyone gets dressed and they all go out. Their friend, Jean
de Brunhoff, has written down a lot of their adventures together and you
can read them with your family while you try out Babar's
favorite brunch recipe:

You'll Need:

1 Loaf thin-sliced white bread

3 to 6 eggs

¼ teaspoon vanilla extract

¼ cup milk

½ teaspoon cinnamon

1 tablespoon sugar

2 tablespoons oil

Powdered sugar

1 cup peanut butter (creamy)

½ cup honey

Skillet or griddle

Mixing bowl

Fork or whisk

Measuring spoons

Measuring cup

Spatula

Clean, empty salt shaker

Before You Cook:

- Measure peanut butter and honey (P & K) into mixing bowl and set aside for topping.
- Fill clean, empty salt shaker with powdered sugar (P & K) and set aside for topping.
- Heat skillet or griddle on medium to medium high heat and coat it with the oil.

Let's Cook!

In the mixing bowl, combine 3 eggs, milk, cinnamon, vanilla, and granulated sugar. Mix with fork or whisk until frothy and lemon-colored (P & K).

Dip bread, one side at a time, in egg mixture coating both sides (K). Put coated slice of bread in hot skillet (P). Flip over when bottom is golden brown and cook the other side

When both sides are browned, put on plate. Sprinkle with powered sugar from shaker and serve or mix peanut butter and honey together and spread on top slice and serve.

Now, gobble it up!

PAUL BUNYAN'S LUMBERJACK
FLAPJACK STACK
(North Woods Pancakes from Scratch)

When Paul Bunyan, the legendary lumberjack, was only two weeks old,
he weighed 100 pounds and for breakfast every day he ate five dozen eggs, 10
sacks of potatoes, and half a barrel of mush made from a whole sack of cornmeal.
If your morning appetite isn't quite that robust, you might want to try the fabu-
lous flapjacks that were served each morning at Paul's
lumber camp on the Big Onion River in Minnesota instead. There were
one thousand of the biggest, strongest lumberjacks in the country at Paul's
camp, and the chow table was so long that it took a week to pass the salt from one
end of the table to the other. Paul's cook, Sourdough Sam,
complained that he could never get seconds ready for the men fast enough and
that it made the boys pretty surly. So, Paul made Sam a flapjack
griddle the size of a skating rink and to grease it, Sourdough Sam had one
hundred men strap bacon fat to the bottoms of their boots and
skate across the hot griddle.
Here's the recipe for those famous flapjacks scaled down a little
so you can make them on your griddle at home:

You'll Need:

2 cups flour
3 teaspoons baking powder
½ teaspoon salt
1 tablespoon sugar
3 tablespoons oil
2 eggs
1⅔ cup milk
½ teaspoon cinnamon

Griddle or skillet
Measuring spoons
Measuring cup
Mixing bowl
Wooden spoon
Spatula
Sifter
Paper towel

Before You Cook:

- Pour 1 tablespoon of oil on the unheated griddle or skillet. Use paper towel to grease the bottom of the skillet or surface of the griddle (K).
- Then preheat the skillet on medium to medium high heat (P).

Let's Cook!

Sift together in the mixing bowl the flour, baking powder, and salt (P & K). Add eggs, milk, sugar, 1 tablespoon of oil and the cinnamon to the bowl (K). Beat with the wooden spoon until all ingredients are combined and batter is smooth **(P)**. Rinse out measuring cup and transfer part of the batter from the bowl to it **(P)**.

Pour batter from the measuring cup on the hot skillet or griddle to form pancakes. Don't pour too much; remember the batter will spread out a little. **(P & K)**. Watch the pancakes carefully. When the top side has bubbles in it, it's time to flip them **(P & K)**. If the pancakes begin to stick to the skillet, use the rest of the oil to re-grease it. To test the second side for doneness, use the spatula to gently lift up the edge of the pancake from the skillet or griddle.

When you see that it's the golden-brown color that you want, it's time to scoop it up with the spatula **(P)** and serve it on a plate, topped with butter and maple syrup.

The batter should make about 24 pancakes for normal people or one gigantic pancake big enough for the lumberjacks at the Big Onion River Camp.

While you're eating this lumberjack breakfast, read the story of how Paul Bunyan met his large friend, Babe, the blue ox. Find out why Paul called him "Babe," and how he got so blue.

GREEN EGGS–HOLD THE HAM

I guess by now everyone has their favorite Dr. Seuss stories—*The Cat in the Hat*, *The Grinch Who Stole Christmas*, *One Fish, Two Fish*—but one of the best-loved is Green Eggs and Ham. This is a particular favorite around my house because my nickname is Sam. I am.

Well, you get the idea...

My children love Dr. Seuss stories, and when they were 3 or 4 years old, I was trying to find a way to get them to eat scrambled eggs. So one morning, I hit on the brilliant idea of making green eggs and ham for breakfast. Or at least it seemed to be a brilliant idea until we were staring at a plate of green ham. YUCK.

So here are some tips we thought we'd pass along to you: first, the best green eggs are scrambled, not fried sunny-side up; second, do NOT attempt to color the ham. Believe me, there's just no way to make ham that color appealing. Now red fish or blue fish...that's a different story....

You'll Need:

Approximately 2 eggs per person
⅓ cup milk

Salt and pepper to taste
2 tablespoons vegetable oil
Green food coloring

Frying pan or skillet
Spatula
Mixing bowl
Fork or whisk

Before You Start:

- Break 8 eggs (this makes 4 portions) into the mixing bowl and dispose of the shells **(P & K)**.
- Use the fork or whisk to beat the eggs until the yolks are broken and mixed with the whites, and are slightly frothy **(P & K)**.

Let's Cook!

Warm the skillet on medium heat with the vegetable oil **(P)**. Add milk to eggs and beat again. Put in about 4 drops of food coloring and beat until you reach the desired color. Add food coloring 1 drop at a time and mix again before adding more until you get to the right color. Do not attempt to make the eggs dark green **(P & K)**.

When the skillet is warm, pour the egg mixture in **(P)**. Stir the eggs around the skillet every few minutes with the spatula or a wooden spoon

(K). Cook until eggs are no longer runny, but do not overcook (if the egg mixture starts to brown, the skillet is too hot or they are over-cooked). Add salt and pepper to taste (P & K) and serve.

While you're enjoying your green eggs and ham, play a game to see who can name the most things that rhyme with Sam. Then try finding Dr. Seuss–type names for objects in the room. For example, we once re-named our old-fashioned egg beater a "two-beater twizdinkular."

Lovable Lunches and
Hiliarious High Tea

If your crew is home, or comes home, for lunches,
following are some ideas, not only to feed everyone, but to keep them
entertained as well. Of course, these ideas can also be adapted
to suppers or snacks in a pinch.

The most important part of these quick meals is actually the story telling.
I have used every tiny opportunity to turn a discussion of a particular story
into the seeds of discovering other similar stories of a certain type of literature. In the case of a "big book" like *Alice's Adventures in Wonderland*, look
over the book and divide it into chapters or sections and read one section
each afternoon or before bedtime at night.

Here are some lovable lunches and one hilarious high tea (which is
traditionally served at 4:00 P.M. — or served at any time convenient to you
by pretending to be a white rabbit who has set his wristwatch
to 4:00 P.M.)....

HEIDI'S HANDKERCHIEF LUNCH

Heidi was a little girl who lived with her grandfather
in the steep hills of Switzerland. Farms in Switzerland hug the sides of the
beautiful, green (and sometimes snow-covered) mountains. Heidi spent
a lot of her time looking after her grandfather's goats, hiking
around these mountains.

As you can imagine, if someone is going to spend a lot of their time
tramping around the Alps, they need a lunch that's high energy and very
portable. My family discovered that it was lots of fun to go on short
explores around the neighborhood carrying lunch Heidi-style in a
bandanna. We'd find a good, secluded spot to break for lunch, and I'd tell
the children about Heidi and her adventures, and about my own visit to
Switzerland and the Alps. Sometimes, we fearless explorers would spend the
trip making our own maps of the undiscovered parts of our neighborhood
and their points of interest.

Switzerland is famous for one of my favorite things: CHOCOLATE. So, it
just wouldn't be a Swiss lunch without some chocolate.

Speaking of chocolate, I once wound up in my car parked on the roof of a
shop that sold Swiss chocolate in Bern, Switzerland. Don't even ask me how
I got there, because I'm still not sure. Here's a quick and easy Heidi-style
lunch (best, of course, when carried around the neighborhood in a
bandanna first and eaten in your own pretend Alps):

You'll Need:

Summer sausage
A block of cheddar cheese
Loaf of French bread or Black bread
A chocolate candy bar
Water

A sharp knife
Zip-seal plastic bags or plastic wrap
A bandanna or scarf
Container for water (plastic bottle or canteen)
Cutting board

Let's Cook!

Use the knife to slice the summer sausage in circles about ¼-inch thick (P). Put a few in each bag, one bag for each hiker (or wrap them tightly in plastic wrap, one package for each hiker) (K).

Next, cut the cheese into slightly thicker slices, about ½- to 1-inch thick. Cut the slices into cubes (P). Get out a bag (or wrap) for each hiker and put 4 to 6 cubes in each bag (K). Tear the bread into hunks, dividing the loaf equally with one piece for each hiker (K). Put bread in bags as above.

With each hiker's stack of food, add one piece of the chocolate in a bag (or one bar apiece, depending upon how much you like chocolate). Lay out each bandanna or scarf flat on the counter or table. Put one bag of sausage, one bag of cheese, one bag of bread and one bag of chocolate in the center of each bandanna. Pull two opposite corners up over the food and tie them in a knot. Pull the other two corners up and tie them in a knot, too (P & K).

Fill canteens or containers with cold water and your lunch is ready to go with you!

SAFETY NOTE:

If it's hot outside, don't wait more than 1 hour to eat your lunch. The sausage and cheese will start to spoil after that and the chocolate will get mooshy.

HEIDI HIKING TIP:

When you're finished with lunch, put empty bags inside one bag, flatten all the air out and stow them in your pocket to throw away at home. Pour a little water from your canteen on the bandanna and tie it loosely around your neck. This will keep you cool on the hottest hike.

Between bites of your Heidi lunch, practice yodeling. People in the Tyrol used to communicate with neighbors by yodeling, which evolved from yelling across valleys. And for more Alpine adventures, read *Heidi* by Johanna Spyri.

TIGER LILY'S TEN LITTLE INDIANS
(A sneaky way to get little brothers and sisters to eat)

In the play "Peter Pan," Sir J.M. Barrie wrote about a boy who ran away to Neverland so he wouldn't ever have to grow up. Peter Pan takes the Darling children, Wendy, Jonathan, and Michael, flying off to his home in Neverland where they meet the Lost Boys, mermaids, Indians, pirates (led by the villainous Captain Hook), and a fairy named Tinkerbell.

The children also meet Peter's good friend, Tiger Lily, who is the daughter of the Indians' chief. They find out that she is very brave herself.

Anytime you have trouble getting your own tribe to sit still and eat, try telling them the story of Peter Pan while making Ten Little Indians.

You'll Need:

1 package hot dogs
1 can shoestring potatoes
Ketchup
½ teaspoon salt

Saucepan for cooking hot dogs
Knife for cutting hot dogs
Fork or cooking tongs

Before You Cook:

• Open the can of shoestring potatoes (P & K).

Let's Cook!

Fill saucepan about three-fourths full of water. Add salt (K). Put water on medium high heat (P). Put hot dogs in water (K). Bring to a rolling boil. Reduce the heat to simmer and let the hot dogs cook approximately 10 to 15 minutes. Remove the pan from the heat. Remove the hot dogs from the water to a plate and let cool slightly (P).

Cut the hot dogs into bite-sized pieces (P if using kitchen knife, K if using plastic "picnic" knife). Serve at least 10 pieces on each person's plate.

Insert a "feather" (shoestring potato) into the flat side of each hot dog bite. Put "war paint" (ketchup) on each plate and serve.

Dip each "Indian" in "war paint" before eating.

While you're cooking this treat, sing the "10 Little Indians" song—a great tune for learning to count—and you might also enjoy doing some detective work when you've finished cooking. Go to your local library to find out which tribe of Native Americans lived or still lives in your area. What were their favorite stories or myths? I always liked Native American stories about Coyote, the Trickster, and the Thunderbird. Check out some of the books about Native American arts like beading, masks or sandpainting, then try drawing some designs of your own.

SAFETY TIP:

Two of the most frequent causes of choking in infants and small children are hot dogs and peanut butter. Make sure "bite-sized" pieces are small enough to prevent these accidents. (Also, your local chapter of the American Red Cross will be happy to give you information or instruction in infant/child Heimlich, First Aid and CPR.)

This might be a good place to mention, too, that First Aid, CPR and storytelling are great skills for potential baby-sitters. This recipe is wonderful for older siblings to prepare with younger brothers and sisters with some supervision. Before my older daughters baby-sat for others, they were required to complete the Junior Girl Scout's "First Aid" and "Child Care" badges and log 20 hours apiece of "practice baby-sitting" with their baby sister.

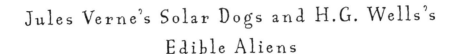

Jules Verne's Solar Dogs and H.G. Wells's Edible Aliens

Do you have a great imagination? Two writers of the late 1800s
and early 1900s, Jules Verne and H.G. Wells, had such terrific imaginations
that they wrote stories about space travel before rockets were invented,
submarines before anyone knew about how to travel under the sea,
and time travel, which still remains to be invented. You could say
they were the "fathers of science fiction."
Jules Verne wrote *From Earth to the Moon* about traveling in space,
and H.G. Wells wrote *The War of the Worlds* about Martians traveling
through space to Earth with the intention of invading and conquering it for
their own hideous reasons. If you feel like eating the Space Age way, how about
building a cooker powered, not by electricity or fuel, like gas, wood, or even
nuclear energy, but by the best-known heat source in our galaxy: the Sun.
The next time you have a hot, sunny afternoon,
try this interstellar lunch:

Solar Dogs
Edible Aliens

Solar Dogs

You'll Need:

1 package beef hot dogs
1 package hot dog buns
Ketchup or mustard

Aluminum foil
Clear, plastic 3-liter soft drink bottle
Sharp craft knife
Clean coat hanger(s)
2 rocks or bricks to hold oven steady

Before You Cook:

- Build you own solar oven: Use a sharp craft knife to cut a flap in one side of the 3 liter soft drink bottle. Put a small hole in the bottom of the bottle, even with the neck of the bottle on the other end **(P)**. Remove any outside labels from the bottle **(K)**.
- Tear off a piece of aluminum foil about the length of the bottle and press it, shiny side up, inside the bottle, opposite the flap you cut in the side **(K)**. Straighten the coat hanger **(P)**.

Let's Cook!

Put one end of the coat hanger through the opening of the bottle. Put 2 hot dogs on the coat hanger (or as many as will fit) lengthwise. Push the end of the coat hanger through the hole in the other end of the bottle **(P & K)**. Close the flap. Brace the oven on a flat surface (like a driveway or sidewalk) with the two rocks or bricks so it will not roll (K).

Now, wait for the sun to do its stuff. Depending on time of year and weather conditions, it takes a while for the dogs to cook. Generally, when they change color and begin to "sweat," you can check them. They'll be warm to the touch. Remove them from the coat hanger put them on a bun with your favorite condiment.

SAFETY TIP:

If the sun isn't cooperative after 1 hour, cook the dogs inside the conventional way and try the solar oven on another day.

These dogs go well with Edible Aliens that you cook in the kitchen while the Solar Dogs cook outside.

Edible Aliens

You'll Need:

8 Alien pods (find them in the grocery store hiding under signs reading
"Brussels Sprouts")—keep them tightly sealed in bag before cooking so
they can't escape
¼ teaspoon salt
Water, enough to almost cover pods

Covered saucepan
Large spoon or ladle

Before You Cook:

• Wash and drain Alien Pods **(P & K).**

Let's Cook!

Put pods in saucepan and add water and salt (P & K). Bring water to a
rolling boil on medium high heat. Cover pan and lower heat to medium
heat. Boil pods approximately 20 minutes or until tender and thoroughly
dead. Add more water during cooking if water begins to boil away.

Remove pods from pan with spoon or ladle and serve with Solar Dogs
(P & K).

Be sure to eat as many Alien Pods as you have cooked; they're sneaky
and sometimes revive in the 'fridge, even after cooking.

THE MAD HATTER'S TEA PARTY

Did you ever have one of those days when everything seems to be topsy-turvy, nothing is what it appears to be and you're either too big or too small? Does it seem that the more you hurry, the later you seem to get? Then you know how Alice and her fantastic friends feel in the books, *Alice's Adventures in Wonderland, Through the Looking Glass,* both written by the English writer Lewis Carroll.

In Wonderland, Alice meets all kinds of interesting and peculiar creatures and people, including a white rabbit who is always late, a disappearing cat with a silly grin, and an exotic but slightly snobby caterpillar, among others.

In the first story, the curious Alice follows a white rabbit wearing a vest and carrying a pocket watch down his rabbit hole to Wonderland. She spends the rest of the story travelling through Wonderland, in and out of adventures, always trying to find her way back to the English garden where she started.

It's a fantastic story, especially considering that it was written by a math teacher.

The only break poor Alice gets is when she comes upon a tea party being given by The Mad Hatter for his guests, The March Hare and a timid Doormouse.

If you'd like to have your own tea party (with or without the Doormouse), here's a good menu to try:

For Tea, You'll Need:

Tea bags
Water
(Ice cubes, if served cold)
Sugar

Tea kettle
Spoon
Large unbreakable container
Large saucepan

For hot tea, by the cup:

Boil water in tea kettle (P). Place tea bag in cup. Pour boiling water over bag and let steep 5 minutes. Remove bag. Add sugar and cinnamon (P & K). Stir.

For iced tea:

Fill saucepan almost full of water (K). Set on medium-high to high heat (P). Boil the water.

Place 4 teabags in boiling water and remove pan from heat (P). Let steep 5-10 minutes. Remove tea bags. Let cool 15 minutes.

Empty ice cube tray into container (K) and pour tea over the ice (P). Add enough water to nearly fill container.

Add sugar and stir until sugar is completely dissolved (P & K).

Refrigerate. Serve over ice cubes and add additional sugar to taste.

For Ribbon Sandwiches, You'll Need:

1 loaf white sandwich bread

Any combination of sandwich ingredients you like, such as:

Cream Cheese (softened or room temperature)

Peanut butter

Jelly

Pimento Cheese spread

Potted Meats (Deviled Ham, for example)

Tuna fish

Bologna, or other lunch meats

Condiments: mayonnaise, salad dressing, mustard, etc.

Butter knife

Plastic wrap

Plate for serving

Let's Cook!

Choose at least 2 sandwich ingredients you think will go together, such as deviled ham and cheese spread.

Cut crusts off of four slices of bread (P). Spread one slice with your choice of condiment (K). Spread deviled ham on that slice. Repeat on second slice using second ingredient (cheese spread). Place one slice on top of the other (P & K). Repeat the process on third and fourth slices (P & K).

Use a sharp knife to cut the bread lengthwise in thirds.

Place sandwiches on serving plate. Repeat the above steps until you have the number of sandwiches you want. Cover sandwiches with plastic wrap and refrigerate until you are ready to serve them.

For Heart Cookies, You'll Need:

2 cups flour

1½ teaspoons baking powder

½ teaspoon salt

½ cup butter or margarine

¾ cup sugar

¾ cup brown sugar

1 egg

1 teaspoon vanilla extract

½ teaspoon cinnamon

Red food coloring (about 4 drops)

Red sugar sprinkles

Mixing bowl

Spoon for stirring

Measuring cup

Measuring spoons

Baking sheet

Rolling pin

Cutting board

Cookie cutter or piece of cardboard and scissors

Small sharp knife

Spatula

Wax paper or foil

NOTE: The dough needs to chill in the refrigerator before being rolled. Either make it the night before (covering the top with wax paper so it doesn't dry out, or put it in the freezer while you make the Ribbon Sandwiches.

Before You Start:

- Preheat the oven to 375°.
- Lightly dust the cutting board with flour. Put a little flour in your hand and dust the rolling pin, turning it until all of it is lightly covered with flour (P & K). If you can't find a heart-shaped cookie cutter, make your own by drawing a heart on the cardboard, then cutting it out with the scissors (P & K).

Let's Cook!

In the mixing bowl, beat together until creamy the butter, sugars, egg, vanilla, and cinnamon (P & K). Add the flour, baking powder, and salt and stir until all ingredients are coated and mixed well (P & K). Add about 4 drops of food coloring and stir it in thoroughly. Add more food coloring, 1 drop at a time, if necessary, until you reach the color you want for the cookies (P & K). Cover the bowl with wax paper and chill in the refrigerator.

When the dough is chilled, turn it onto your lightly floured board and roll out the dough to a thickness of about $\frac{1}{8}$ inch (P & K). Cut the cookies into heart shapes and place on the baking sheet (P & K). If using the cardboard cutter, put the pattern on the dough and trace around it with a small, sharp knife (P). Sprinkle the red sugar crystals on each heart on the baking sheet. Bake each sheet for 8 to 10 minutes, but don't let the edges get crispy and brown. Remove the sheet from the oven (P). Use the spatula to remove the cookies from the sheet (P & K) right away and put them on a cooling rack (P & K).

Set your table for the tea party and serve everyone. If you want to make it more like the Mad Hatter's Tea Party, try telling riddles. The Mad Hatter and the March Hare didn't think Alice was very good at riddling. See how many riddles you can guess.

SAFETY TIP:

It is not a particularly good idea to invite Jabberwockies to tea parties.

Delicious Dinners

Dinners, of course, take time. But one way around the time drain that preparing dinner puts on your day is to combine it with more than one activity and include everyone available.

While a parent is chopping, boiling, or sautéing, the other family members can be doing homework or helping others with their homework, talking about their day, or telling the stories that go with that particular recipe.

This is also a great time, I've found, for turning off the television in the other room and sharing different kinds of music. Please remember that this a give-take situation; if you play "Peter and the Wolf" or "Carnival of the Animals" for them, it's only fair that you listen to the latest boy group or metal band. And one of the largest stumbling blocks in family communication that I've noticed lately is that as soon as we, as grown-ups, begin writing checks for the monthly rent we somehow magically forget what it was like to be 6, 10, or 14. Young people have problems and concerns, likes and dislikes, and these are just as important to them as our job or debt problems are to us.

One of the most rewarding and stress-reducing things adults can do is "travel back." Kids love to hear how much your parents hated your music, the most embarrassing thing that ever happened to you in school, or what your favorite book, movie, or TV show was when you were small.

It's also hard to believe, I know, but eventually, after you've tried these menus more than once and as your helpers get bigger, preparing a meal together actually speeds up preparation time, and having two, three, or four extra pairs of hands in the kitchen will give you more time to spend together on other things.

Have fun preparing and sharing these Delicious Dinners....

THREE BEARS' PORRIDGE

On a nippy day or whenever the world is getting to be too much for me,
I know exactly why Papa and Baby Bear loved for Mama Bear to make a big
kettle of porridge for them. You can make it fancier by sprinkling fresh,
chopped chives on top when you serve it, or give it a more distinctive taste by
adding $1/4$ teaspoon of garlic with the rest of the seasonings. You can also adjust
the consistency (thicker or "soup-ier") by boiling the potatoes longer until they
are falling apart (thicker) or for a briefer time, until the potatoes cut easily
with the side of a fork (thinner). Keep in mind that when you lower the heat to
add the other ingredients, the potatoes stop cooking for the most part
and stay at that consistency.

Just a quick note here: Most people do not know that Mama Bear is actually of
Irish descent. Her family emigrated from Ireland to America about 1842, during The Great Potato Famine and Bear Emigration. They settled originally in
Idaho, the Potato State. Her family gradually moved across the country to
Wyoming, just outside Yellowstone Park, near the Snake River, where they
became locally famous as entertainers, posing for pictures for tourists. It was
during a summer job showing park visitors the way to the entrance of
Yellowstone Park that Mama Bear first met Papa Bear, who also had a
summer job demonstrating bear trout-fishing techniques.

Even Mama Bear herself admits, by the way, that the porridge she made the day
that Goldilocks came by was not one of her best batches. If it had been, she says,
Goldilocks would still be sitting at the dining room table slurping it up, and
they might have avoided the whole ugly chair breaking, bed bouncing mess.

Baby Bear also told me that Mama Bear did make her usual
great gooey Grilled Cheese Sandwiches that day, but not until "that scary little
girl," as he calls Goldilocks, was gone.

You'll Need:

4 to 6 medium potatoes

Water to cover potatoes

Salt and pepper to taste

1 can condensed milk

1 medium onion

½ cup margarine

2 quart saucepan or soup kettle or small Dutch oven (anything that can comfortably hold potatoes and liquids)

Small, sharp knife

Potato peeler (optional)

Wooden spoon or other big spoon for stirring

Cutting board

Can opener

Measuring cup

Before You Cook:

- Peel and wash potatoes. If you use a potato peeler, this is a (K). If your family uses a small, sharp knife, called a paring knife, this is a (P). Washing the potatoes is a (K).
- Do not put potato peels in a garbage disposal.
- Cut the potatoes into rough cubes, about 1 to 1½ inches. This is a (P).
- Peel and wash the onion. Peeling is a (P), washing is a (K).
- Cut the onion into pieces about the same size as the potatoes. This is a (P).
- Open the can of condensed milk (whole milk can be used in a pinch, but the soup will taste "thinner" and you must watch the temperature closely. If it gets too hot, the milk clots and curdles and tastes sour. Yuck!)
- Measure the margarine and have it ready.

Let's Cook!

Put the potato and onion pieces in the saucepan. Cover the potatoes with water. Add salt and pepper to taste. (At one time, my children thought black pepper looked like "dirt" in the soup. I made the soup with white pepper until everybody got over it.)

Put the saucepan on a large burner and cook over medium high heat. Boil potatoes and onions until desired consistency is reached. (While the potatoes and onions boil, you can get things ready for the Grilled Cheese Sandwiches.) The easiest way to test the potatoes is to have a **P** scoop out a potato with the stirring spoon and put it on the cutting board or a small saucer. Cut it with the side of the spoon or a fork. It should cut easily or crumble when it's ready, depending upon what consistency you want the porridge. Add water as necessary during the boiling to keep the potatoes covered. *Do not let the potatoes scorch.* Burnt potatoes smell *awful.*

When the potatoes are ready, reduce heat to low or simmer. Add margarine and milk and stir **(K).** Adjust salt and pepper to taste. Let the porridge simmer until it "seasons," about 30 minutes. (This is a good time to start on the Grilled Cheese Sandwiches if you are having them with the porridge.) If the porridge begins to reduce, add a little water. Be sure to stir before serving.

Serve and enjoy while telling the story of "Goldilocks and the Three Bears" using a different voice for each character.

BABY BEAR'S GOOEY GRILLED CHEESE SANDWICHES
(For Un-Bear-Ably Big Appetites)

You'll Need:

1 loaf thinly-sliced white sandwich bread
Margarine or butter
Cheddar or Colby cheese

Knife for cutting
Knife for spreading
Skillet or griddle
Spatula
Cutting board

Before You Cook:

- P needs to cut approximately 2 slices of cheese for each sandwich.
- K needs to count 2 slices of bread for each sandwich. Heat skillet or griddle on medium heat.

Let's Cook!

Spread butter or margarine on one side of bread (K). Put one slice butter side down in skillet. Place slices of cheese on the bread. Place another slice of bread, butter side up, on top of the cheese.

Check the bottom slice. When it turns golden brown, flip with spatula (P or K).

Repeat the process for this side, then serve.

RED RIDINGHOOD'S BASKET OF GOODIES
(A Picnic Supper for Indoors or Outdoors)

World's Easiest Baked Chicken
Breadsticks
Grapes
Carrot Sticks
Apple Juice

When I was a very little girl, the only story the adults in my life
seemed to know by heart was the story of *Little Red Ridinghood*. They told it
with a great deal of enthusiasm, different character voices and so often that by
the time I was five, I was pretty convinced that 1. adults are a bit dull no matter
how hard they try to be entertaining and 2. there is something incredibly
sinister about picking flowers.
Now that I'm an adult myself, I realize that those were just the observations of
an unsophisticated and childish mind, and that 1. adults often get a bad wrap
from their small charges and 2. there is something incredibly
sinister about picking flowers.
I've never really figured out the ominous flower-picking thing. Never.
On the other hand, since everyone is so familiar with the story,
when you tell it or read it together, each person can enjoy taking a part or
helping with the part of the story they like best. Your family can have some fun
making and packing up Little Red Ridinghood's basket of goodies to take on
an early evening picnic to a local park or through your pretend
forest at home to your picnic site in the backyard
or the living room.

For Baked Chicken, You'll Need:

1 2- to 3-pound chicken, whole fryer
Season salt

Pan for the oven with at least a 2-inch lip, large enough
for baking rack to fit into
Baking rack
Aluminum foil
Cutting board
Sharp knife for cutting chicken

Before You Start:

- Preheat the oven to 350°.
- Line the bottom of the pan with aluminum foil. Set the rack inside the pan (P & K).
- Wash and clean the chicken inside and out with hot water and mild liquid dishwashing soap. Rinse thoroughly (P). Chicken can be left whole or cut into pieces. To cut the chicken, begin with wings and cut at joints closet to the body. Next, cut thighs and legs as whole pieces (P). Place these 4 pieces on the rack. Then, cut horizontally through chest cavity under ribs from front to rear. Place knife blade along the backbone and trim off one side of the breast, then repeat the process on the opposite side of the backbone (P). Place the breasts on the rack. Wrap and discard carcass immediately or put into stock pot to boil down for chicken stock.

Let's Cook!

Sprinkle seasoned salt on chicken and rub in lightly until chicken is covered. Turn pieces over and season the other side (P & K). Arrange pieces on baking rack over pan so none of the pieces hang over the edge. Carefully place pan in oven. Bake chicken at 350° for about 1 hour to 1 hour and 30 minutes until the inside of the chicken is thoroughly cooked and the juices run clear.

While the chicken is baking, prepare breadsticks and other goodies.

For Breadsticks, You'll Need:

¼ cup butter or margarine
2 cups powdered biscuit mix
1 tablespoon sugar
½ cup milk
½ cup grated parmesan cheese
¼ teaspoon oregano

Spatula
Wire rack
Bowl for mixing
Measuring spoons
Measuring cup
Spoon for mixing
Baking sheet with lip
Cutting board
Sharp knife
Pastry brush or clean paint brush

Before You Cook:

- Preheat the oven to 400°.
- Put butter in a baking pan and place in the oven just until melted (P).

Let's Cook!

In mixing bowl, stir together biscuit mix, sugar, milk, cheese, and oregano (P & K). Stir until dough is stiff, then dust cutting board lightly with biscuit mix and turn dough onto board (P & K). Knead the dough by folding one corner into the center and pressing down with heel of your hand (P & K). Fold next corner into the middle of dough and press down. Repeat with the other two corners. Repeat this process nine more times (P & K).

Roll out dough on cutting board into a roughly rectangular shape, about 12 x 8 inches. Use knife to cut dough in half. Cut each half into strips approximately 1½ to 2 inches wide. Roll each strip on cutting board with fingers like rolling a snake out of clay. Place strip on baking sheet and use brush to coat with melted butter (P & K).

Put the baking sheet in the oven (P) and bake for approximately 10 to 12 minutes until golden brown.

Remove the sheet from the oven and put the breadsticks on a wire baking rack to cool (K).

For Other Goodies, You'll Need:

1 to 2 pounds seedless grapes
1 bag carrots
1 small container of Ranch or Green Onion dip

Bowl for serving
Colander
Peeler or paring knife
Knife
Plate for serving

Before You Start:

- Pare or scrape carrot **(K)**. Wash and cut off both ends. Use knife to cut carrots into pieces about 3 inches long **(P)**. Cut each piece of carrot into 4 smaller strips **(P)**.
- Wash grapes thoroughly and put in colander to drain.

Let's Cook!

Place opened dip in center of serving plate and surround with carrot slices.

Make sure grapes are dry then place in serving bowl.

Pour cooled apple juice in glasses **(P & K)**. Cut chicken into pieces for serving **(P)**. Spread out blanket or tablecloth on the floor and serve chicken, grapes and carrot sticks **(P & K)**.

Decide which version of Little Red Ridinghood you like best and tell it while "picnicking." This is also a good springboard to use to talk to younger children about stranger safety in a non-threatening way.

BILBO BAGGINS'S ELEVENTY-FIRST BIRTHDAY DINNER
(Especially good when served September 23rd, the little guy's actual birth date)

Hobbit Stew
Shire Cakes

Hobbits are delightful little creatures to invite to any party. They are between three and four feet tall and don't wear shoes because they have very furry feet. They also love to cook, they love to eat and drink, and are rumored to have quite a sweet tooth. Hobbits are fun at parties because they're fond of singing and music, and entertain their families and friends by writing and reciting very exciting poetry. Among their acquaintances, they count wizards, dwarfs, elves, and even people.

You can imagine how festive their birthday parties are. A man named J.R.R. Tolkien wrote about the hobbits and all the inhabitants of Middle Earth in his books. In *Fellowship of the Ring,* he writes about the eleventy-first (111st) birthday party of one of the most famous (or is it infamous?) hobbits of all, Mr. Bilbo Baggins.

Now, you and I could probably never prepare all of the food from the usual hobbit feast because they consume so much, but I will be happy to share the portion of the menu that my children like best on September 23rd, Bilbo Baggins's birthday.

For Hobbit Stew, You'll Need:

2 pounds of beef, cubed

Approximately ½ cup flour

1 cup beef bouillon (1 cup water, 2 bouillon cubes)

1 cup tomato sauce

12 whole peppercorns

3 bay leaves

3 whole cloves

1 small onion

3 medium potatoes

3 carrots

2 stalks of celery

1 tablespoon oil

Skillet

Large sauce pan or soup kettle with lid

Wooden spoon

Knife for cutting beef and vegetables

Cutting board

Measuring spoons

Measuring cup

Tea kettle

Bowl for bouillon (not metal or glass)

Can opener

Before You Cook:

• Boil 1 C. water in tea kettle on medium high heat to make beef bouillon (P & K). Peel the potatoes and carrots (K). Wash the vegetables and cut the celery and onion into pieces (P).

• Cube the beef (P).

• Open the tomato sauce and set it aside (K).

Let's Cook!

Put oil in skillet and set on medium heat. Brown beef cubes on all sides (P). Remove meat from heat and sprinkle with flour, turning the pieces to lightly coat them (P & K). Set meat aside.

Combine in the large sauce pan the bouillon, tomato sauce, onion, cloves, bay leaves, and peppercorns and put on medium high heat (P & K). When mixture boils add meat to sauce pan and reduce heat to low (P & K). Put lid on sauce pan and simmer for 2 to 3 hours.

The last hour the mixture is simmering, add potatoes, carrots, and celery (P & K).

While the stew is simmering, make Shire Cakes.

For Shire Cakes, You'll Need:

1 package cake mix
(or 1 cup white cake flour, 1 cup Whole wheat flour,
½ teaspoon salt, and 2 teaspoons baking powder)
½ cup butter or margarine
Container of your favorite frosting
1¼ cup sugar
2 eggs
1 cup milk
1 teaspoon vanilla extract
⅛ teaspoon allspice
Shelled pecan halves (optional)

Knife for spreading frosting
2 mixing bowls
Measuring spoons
Measuring cup
Mixer
Spoon for stirring
Paper or foil baking cups
Muffin pan

Before You Cook:

- If using cake mix, follow the package directions.
- If baking from scratch: Preheat the oven to 375°.
- Put baking cups in muffin pan (K).

Let's Cook!

In one bowl, combine flour, salt and baking powder (P & K). In the other bowl, cream the butter until it is smooth (P). Add the sugar to the butter (K) and beat until they're light and fluffy (P). Add one egg to the butter and sugar and beat it thoroughly. Do the same with the second egg.

Pour a little of the flour mixture from the other bowl into the batter and make sure it is well mixed. Add a bit of the milk and stir it in. Add more flour and stir, then more of the milk and stir (P & K). Repeat until all of the flour mixture and milk have been used.

Stir in the vanilla and allspice (P & K).

Use the spoon to ladle the batter into the baking cups in the muffin pan (P & K). Cups should be about three-fourths full.

Put the pan in the oven and bake about 20 minutes (P). Test by inserting a toothpick into the center of the cupcake (K). When it comes out without crumbs or batter sticking to it, the cupcakes are ready.

Remove the pan from the oven (P) and carefully move the cupcakes to a wire rack to cool (P & K).

When cupcakes are completely cooled, spread the top with your favorite frosting (P & K). If you like, put half of a pecan in the middle of the frosting.

Serve big bowls of Hobbit Stew after removing and discarding the bay leaves, cloves, and peppercorns. After the stew, serve the Shire Cakes, and if you're serving them on September 23rd, add a birthday candle and sing "Happy Birthday" to Bilbo.

One of my favorite memories of my children's early years is the whole family piled on the master bed, scattered this way and that way on their favorite pillows in nightgowns and pajamas to listen to me read *The Hobbit* by J.R.R. Tolkien. All winter, we read one chapter a night, and even though I thought they'd fallen sound asleep before the end of a chapter once in a while, they'd surprise me the next night by remembering exactly where we had left off the night before. One thing that amazed me when I read the story out loud was how exciting it is for young children. We spent all winter following Bilbo, the brave hobbit, from his cozy house in the Shire, through all his adventures in Middle Earth. I can definitely recommend this method of warming your home in cold months.

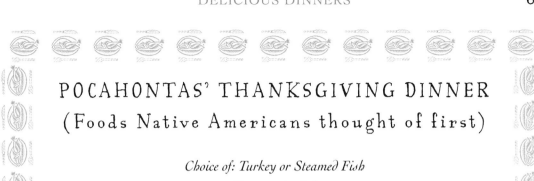

POCAHONTAS' THANKSGIVING DINNER
(Foods Native Americans thought of first)

Choice of: Turkey or Steamed Fish
Corn on the Cob
Baked Potato
Peanut Butter and Chocolate Drop Cookies

Native American culture is incredibly rich and colorful.
Long before the Europeans sailed to North America, Native Americans had a thriving civilization with a strong connection to the Earth and Nature. While the early settlers in the Americas were battling the elements, the Native Americans had already learned to live in harmony with the seasons. Many people are surprised to find out that some of your favorite foods came from Native American societies in North and South America—chocolate, peanuts, pumpkin, turkey, corn and potatoes were served by Native Americans first.

Our Thanksgiving Day is based on the story of settlers
in Plymouth, having survived their first traumatic winter in America, giving thanks by serving a harvest feast. They invited their neighbors, probably a tribe of the Iroquois League, to share their banquet. Their guests brought with them foods native to America.

We know the first Thanksgiving was celebrated in 1622 and that George Washington was the first president to declare it a national holiday.
I always wondered if Pocahontas, the daughter of Chief Powhatan, helped to serve a later Thanksgiving dinner at the Jamestown settlement with her English husband, John Rolfe. Here's a menu for your family to try on this day of thanks, but while you're cooking it, don't forget your thanks to the culture that introduced these "American" foods to the pilgrims.

If You Are Making A Turkey, You'll Need:

A frozen turkey
Butter
2 Large onions
2 to 3 Stalks of celery
10 Whole cloves

A large roasting pan
A wire rack that fits inside the roaster
Pastry brush or clean paint brush
Bowl
Cutting board
Sharp knife

Before You Cook:

- Thaw the frozen turkey in the bottom of the refrigerator for 1 to 2 days, depending on its size. Make sure it is completely thawed before cooking.
- When thawed, clean out the inner cavity of the bird, removing giblets, heart, lungs, etc. and wash inside and outside of the bird thoroughly (P).
- Wash and peel onions. Separate and wash celery stalks (K).
- Preheat the oven to 450°.

Let's Cook!

Cut off the tips and bottoms of the celery (P). Chop the celery, including the leaves (P) and stuff inside the turkey (K). Push the cloves into the onions (K) and put the onions inside the turkey (K).

Place the rack inside the roasting pan and put the turkey on the rack, breast side up (P).

Put the roasting pan in the oven and immediately turn the heat down to 350° (P).

If the turkey is under 18 pounds, cook 20 minutes per pound at 350°. If it is 18 to 25 pounds, cook 15 minutes per pound at 300°.

Baste the turkey frequently throughout the cooking, about every 15 minutes (P & K).

Halfway through the cooking, remove the roaster from the oven and carefully turn the turkey breast side down on the rack and return it to the oven to continue cooking. The turkey is done when you make a small cut on the thigh or prick it with a meat fork and the juices run clear (P & K).

When done, remove the turkey from the oven and place it on a platter or cutting board to carve. Remove celery and onions from inside the bird and discard them (P & K).

SAFETY TIP:

Like chicken, safe handling of a turkey requires thoroughly cleaning the bird, your hands and all surfaces, like cutting boards, before and after cooking. Several studies have shown that, if you like dressing or stuffing with turkey, it is safer, health wise, to cook the stuffing separately from the turkey instead of inside it.

If Your Main Course Is Fish, You'll Need:

Any white fish (cod, catfish, or trout, for example), enough fillets
or portions for one per person
1 large lemon
1 large onion
Butter or margarine

Aluminum foil
Cutting board
Sharp knife

Before You Cook:

- Wash and peel the onion (P & K).
- Wash fish fillets and pat them dry with paper towels (P & K).
- Preheat the oven to 350°.
- Cut the lemon and onion into thin, round slices (P), and set aside.

Let's Cook!

Tear off one piece of foil for each fillet long enough to fold completely
around fish and turn down a seam at the top and sides (K).

Using fingers, butter the inside of the foil (K).

Place 1 or 2 rings of the onion on each piece of buttered foil. Put a slice
of lemon on top of the onions. Next, place the fish length-wise on top of the
onion and lemon. Dot the fish with small pieces of butter (P & K).

Fold the foil up around the fish and turn down the top seam. Seal both
ends toward the middle of the packet (K).

Place the fish in the oven and bake approximately 18 minutes (P). Fish should be tender but not mushy when done.

When done, remove foil packets from the oven and unfold foil. Serve fish on plates and use lemon and onions for garnish (P & K).

For Baked Potatoes, You'll Need:

1 Medium to large baking potato per person

Aluminum foil

Before You Cook:

- Wash the potatoes.
- Preheat the oven to 350°.

Let's Cook!

Using your hands spread oil on the outside of the potatoes to coat them (K).

Tear off a piece of foil for each potato large enough to wrap all the way around potato (K).

Place a potato in the middle of each piece of foil. Fold the foil around each potato and seal the ends (K).

Put covered potatoes in the oven and bake for 1 hour (P).

When done, remove from the oven and unwrap (P). Split with a knife and fill with your choice of condiments and seasonings (P).

For Corn on the Cob, You'll Need:

1 to 2 ears of corn per person
Water
Seasonings to taste
Butter or margarine

Steamer
Tongs
Sharp knife
Cutting board

Before You Cook:

- Pull the husks and silks off of ears and discard (P & K).
- Wash the corn thoroughly.

Let's Cook!

Fill the bottom of steamer three-fourths full with water. Add salt and pepper to the water.

Cut off the tops of the corn cobs. Cut the ears in half. Place the corn in the top of the steamer and cover (P).

Put steamer together and place on the burner to cook over medium high heat (K). Steam until the corn kernels are tender when poked with a fork. Check the water occasionally to make sure it doesn't boil away. Add more water if necessary.

When the corn is done, remove the ears with tongs (P) and serve with skewers for corn in each end to hold onto. Add butter and salt and pepper to taste.

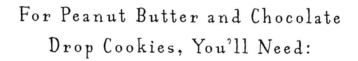

For Peanut Butter and Chocolate Drop Cookies, You'll Need:

2 cups sugar

½ cup cocoa

½ cup butter or margarine

½ cup milk

½ cup smooth peanut butter

3 cups quick-cooking oats

1 teaspoon vanilla extract

Measuring cup

Measuring spoons

Medium-sized sauce pan

Long wooden spoon

Waxed paper

Spoons for "dropping" dough

Trivet

Before You Cook:

- Cover a long counter or tabletop near the stove with waxed paper (P & K).
- Have spoons ready.

Let's Cook!

In the sauce pan, on medium to medium-high heat, stir together sugar, cocoa, butter, milk, and peanut butter (P & K). Bring to a rolling boil, stirring frequently (P). Add oats and mix well (P & K).

Take sauce pan off the burner and quickly stir in vanilla **(P)**. Set sauce pan on trivet near waxed paper.

Use regular teaspoons (2 per person), one to scoop mixture up and the back of the other one to scrape mixture by drops onto the waxed paper **(P & K)**.

Let mixture cool. When set, remove cookies from paper and set on serving plate **(P & K)**. These cookies are fast and fun, but can be slightly temperamental when it comes to setting up properly. Try the cookie recipe before serving them "officially" with the above menu. Humidity, temperature of the kitchen and even brand of peanut butter can affect the end result. If you have trouble getting them to set, try adding more oatmeal, about ½ cup at a time or using a little less milk. On the good side, the mistakes are fun to eat with a spoon.

PINOCCHIO'S PUPPET STRINGS

Pinocchio's Puppet Strings with Sauce (Spaghetti)
Easy Garlic Bread

When I was small, I always thought of *Pinocchio* as being one of the
more hair-raising fairy tales. And to a child's mind that sees the world in terms
of black and white, good and evil, I didn't know what to make of a story in which
the hero lied, skipped school, and ran away from home.

Talk about a morality tale! An acquaintance of mine told me that
his mother could always tell when he was being less that truthful as a small boy.
He thought she had some sort of supernatural radar until she finally told him as
an adult that after he'd seen the Disney version of Pinocchio as a child she
noticed that every time he told a fishy story he would unconsciously
touch the end of his nose to see if it had grown.

Since *Pinocchio* is essentially an Italian fairy tale, here's a dinner menu
that's quick and easy and leaves your family with enough time to read this
and other stories after dinner.

For Puppet Strings And Garlic Bread, You'll Need:

1 package spaghetti or vermicelli noodles

1 jar spaghetti sauce

Oil

1 slice sandwich bread for each person

Butter or margarine

Garlic Salt

Salt

Water

Large saucepan

Medium saucepan

Colander for draining

Knife for spreading

Ladle

Baking Sheet

Spatula

Measuring spoons

Before You Cook:

- Put 6 to 8 cups of water and ¼ teaspoon salt in the large sauce pan. Put sauce pan on the burner on a medium-high heat and let it come to a boil (P & K).
- Set the oven on broil and leave the oven door ajar.

Let's Cook!

Open the spaghetti sauce and put it in the medium sauce pan (K). Place the sauce pan on a burner set on a low to medium heat (P).

When the water comes to a boil in the other sauce pan, add the noodles (P & K). Stir in 1 tablespoon of oil and let cook approximately 10 minutes, stirring occasionally to keep the noodles from sticking to the pan (P & K).

While the noodles and sauce cook, spread one side of each slice of bread with butter (K). Sprinkle each slice very lightly with garlic salt (P & K). Place slices, butter side up, on the baking sheet (P & K). Put the baking sheet in the oven under the broiler element, about 2 minutes, or until the edges of the bread become slightly browned (P). Remove the sheet from the oven, and turn off the broiler. Cut each slice into three parts lengthwise (P).

When the spaghetti is tender, pour it into the colander in the sink to drain. You may also add 1 tablespoon of butter and ½ teaspoon of garlic salt to the noodles and toss them gently

Put a serving of noodles on each plate and use the ladle to cover them with sauce (P & K). Place garlic bread on each plate and serve (P & K).

It might be fun to talk about the fact that everyone thinks of spaghetti as being Italian, even though it originated some place else. Talk about Marco Polo—when and where he lived, the route he followed while exploring, the new discoveries he brought home with him and what happened when he got home.

This is also a great start for a discussion of explorers and geography, as well as how your ancestors came to live in the U.S.

THE BABY-SITTERS CLUB
SLUMBER PARTY

Designer Pizza
Crunchy Munchies
Indoor S'Mores

There is really no way of describing a slumber party of 8 or 10 pre-teens
or teenagers; it's just one of those things you have to experience for yourself.
I recommend keeping the menu fun and simple...and plentiful,
as girls seem to go through what I always thought of as the "piranha phase,"
when they eat everything in your house except the furniture and
they only stop there because they suspect that Scotchguard
might be good for them.
One thing that rings so true in the Baby-sitters Club books is that when a
number of girls get together, there is no stopping them.
Keep them busy and everyone will be happy.
Here's a menu for a slumber party that gets all your guests involved
in cooking as well as eating.
Designer Pizza is simply a pizza (or two or three, depending on age, appetite
and number of guests) that everyone gets to customize.

For Each Pizza, You'll Need:

1 package yeast

½ cup warm water

1½ cups flour

½ teaspoon salt

1 teaspoon sugar

1 tablespoon oil

1 jar pizza or spaghetti sauce

1 cup grated mozzarella cheese

1 onion

1 can pitted black olives

1 package sliced pepperoni

1 green bell pepper

1 4-ounce can whole mushrooms

½ pound hamburger

Optional Ingredients:

Canadian bacon

Italian sausage

Anchovies

Pineapple

Green olives

Red and yellow peppers

Pizza pan or round baking sheet

Pizza cutter

Sharp knife

1 small bowl

1 large mixing bowl

Fork for stirring
Clean kitchen towel
Can opener
Skillet
Cutting boards

Before You Cook:

- Preheat the oven to 450°.
- Use the oil to generously grease the pizza pan (K).
- Brown the hamburger in a skillet, drain the fat off, set aside (P).
- Chop onion, olives, peppers, and mushroom and any of the optional ingredients you choose (P & K). Put them on a plate so everyone can get to them easily.

Let's Cook!

In the small bowl, combine yeast, warm water, and sugar. Stir gently. Let rest about 10 minutes (P).

In the larger bowl mix the flour and salt. Add the yeast mixture and stir lightly with the fork. When all ingredients have been mixed, they form a sticky ball. Pour 1 tablespoon of oil over the top of the dough, then turn the dough in the bowl until it is coated on the outside with oil. Cover the bowl with the towel to prevent drafts and let dough rest 10 minutes (P & K).

After the dough has rested, put it in the center of the pizza pan and press lightly with oiled hands until flattened to fill the entire pan (P & K).

Open the spaghetti sauce and using a spoon or ladle, apply to the crust until you have a light layer of sauce all the way to the rim of the pan (K). Sprinkle mozzarella generously over the entire pizza (P & K). Then use the pizza cutter to very lightly score the pizza into 8 sections (P). Everybody puts the ingredients they want on their own slice or slices (K).

Put the pizza pan in the oven and bake for about 20 minutes until the crust browns and the cheese melts completely **(P)**.

While the pizza cooks, prepare the Crunchy Munchies.

For Crunchy Munchies, You'll Need:

1 bunch of celery
1 bag of carrots
1 container ripe strawberries
4 apples
Chocolate syrup
1 small brick of cream cheese
1 container of Ranch or green onion dip
Honey
Peanut butter

Peeler or sharp knife for paring
Sharp knife for cutting
Large serving plate, platter or tray
Small sauce cups or bowls

Before You Cook:
- Wash all the fruits and vegetables **(K)** and cut off tops and tips.
- Core the apples **(P)**.

Let's Cook!

One group can cut the celery into pieces about 3 inches long, cut the carrots into pieces the same size, then into strips, cut the strawberries in half and the apples into eighths **(P & K)**.

Another group can fill the sauce bowls for dipping with dip, honey, peanut butter and cream cheese **(P & K)**.

Put all of the above on a large platter and serve with Designer Pizza.

When the initial feeding frenzy is over and everyone wants dessert, start on the Indoor S'Mores.

For Indoor S'Mores, You'll Need:

1 box graham crackers
10 plain chocolate bars
1 bag large marshmallows

Baking sheet
Spatula
Lots of paper towels

Before You Cook:

- Make sure an adult is in charge of the oven. Set the oven on broil **(P)**.
- Break graham crackers in half so each person has two pieces. Unwrap chocolate bars and break them approximately into thirds **(K)**.

Let's Cook!

Build the s'mores on the baking sheet by placing one piece of graham cracker on the sheet, one piece of chocolate on top of the cracker and a marshmallow on top of the chocolate. Next to this, place the other piece of graham cracker and another piece of chocolate on top of it **(K)**.

When you have one of each piece for each person, slide the baking sheet into the oven, leaving the oven door ajar while the broiler is on **(P)**.

Remove the baking sheet when the tops of the marshmallows turn a light golden brown (P).

Use the spatula to remove the pieces from the sheet and put them on a clean plate or dry cutting board (P).

Each person places the graham square with chocolate only on top of the other graham square, chocolate side down and presses lightly (K).

Distribute paper towels or lots of napkins, as these are both scrumptious and gooey.

Depending on the age and size of your slumber party group, some fun things to keep them occupied are:

A Barbie Fashion Show
- Everyone dresses her Barbie in 5 minutes, then makes two lines facing each other on the floor. Put on some 50's rock 'n roll or 80's disco while each Barbie "walks" down the center, between the two lines, doing The Stroll to show off her outfit.

A Baby-sitters Club Mystery
- Before the party, decide on a mystery (i.e. Dawn has lost her favorite ring) and it's up to the party-goers to solve it. Using index cards, hide the written clues around the house or yard. Each card gives a clue that leads to the next clue. The final destination can be the location of your party favors, the birthday presents or another surprise. If you're using the ring mystery, the last clue leads to a "treasure chest" containing party favor rings for each guest.

Twister
- Still the big favorite for slumber parties and takes on a different challenge for each age group. Younger players are so short they have to stretch and taller, gawkier players get more easily tangled up.

YANKEE DOODLE'S
ALL-AMERICAN DINNER

Hamburgers
Macaroni and Cheese
Peas or vegetable of choice
Juice Popsicles

Any parent knows that small children love the rhythmic repetitions of nursery rhymes and simple songs. Especially the repetition part.

What loving parent hasn't been driven stark raving mad on a rainy afternoon by one or more small children gleefully singing "London Bridge" or "Yankee Doodle" 261 times in a row?

One of the first rhymes children learn is Yankee Doodle and, as an informed parent who has done quite a bit of reading on child psychology, my own theory is that the reason children love this particular song so much is that it mentions macaroni. Macaroni appears to be to toddlers and young children what ambrosia was to the ancient gods of Mt. Olympus.

Repetition appeals to children because it gives them a sense of practicing something until they conquer it, and repetition of certain menus on certain days seems to give them a sense of security. When I was small, it was a meal of spaghetti and peas on Wednesday nights and my children are still convinced that the weekend cannot begin without homemade pizza on Friday night.

Here is an all-American dinner menu for your family night that includes, of course, macaroni. This is a simple, quick menu composed mainly of convenience foods so you'll have more time to read nursery rhymes.

You'll Need:

1 to 2 pounds ground hamburger (enough to form at least one patty
for each diner)
1 small onion
1 teaspoon Worcestershire sauce
1 package hamburger buns
1 package macaroni and cheese dinner
1 to 2 cans peas, or favorite vegetable
1 64-ounce bottle or can of your favorite fruit juice

Mixing bowl
Skillet
Spatula
Sharp knife
Measuring spoons
Large sauce pan
Medium sauce pan
Can opener

Colander for draining noodles
1 package small disposable cups
1 package craft sticks
Spoon for stirring

Before You Cook:

The day before you plan to serve this meal, make the juice popsicles. Set
out a paper cup for each person and fill it approximately three-fourths full
of fruit juice (P & K). Put the cups in the freezer. After 45 minutes to 1

hour, place a clean craft stick in each cup and let the popsicles set until after your dinner. These work best when you use cups that are coated with wax.

When you're ready to prepare the meal wash and peel the onion.

Let's Cook!

Put the hamburger in a mixing bowl and use your clean hands to break up the meat (P & K).

Chop the onion and add it to the meat, along with the Worcestershire sauce (P & K). Use hands to mix these ingredients thoroughly (K).

Put skillet on one burner and add oil. Put the large sauce pan on another burner. Add 6 to 8 cups water to sauce pan and ¼ teaspoon salt to water (P & K). Warm skillet on medium heat and sauce pan on medium-high heat until water boils.

Form balls out of hamburger, then use your palm to flatten them into patties (P & K). Place as many patties as will comfortably fit into the skillet (P). If all patties are not cooked at one time, put the remaining patties on a plate, cover them with foil or plastic wrap and put them in the refrigerator until you are ready to cook them.

When the water boils in the sauce pan, add the macaroni noodles and 1 tablespoon of oil and stir (P & K). Follow package directions.

While the noodles and burgers cook, open the vegetable (K) and put a small sauce pan on a burner (K). Put the vegetable in the sauce pan and set on low heat (P & K). Add the seasonings you prefer and stir (P & K).

Cook the hamburgers for approximately 5 to 10 minutes on the first side, then use a spatula to turn them (P). Cook second side until juices rise on the top, then flip again and cook briefly (P). Inside should be barely pink. Use spatula to remove burger from skillet to a hamburger bun (P) and add condiments and garnish as you prefer (K).

Serve the burgers, macaroni and cheese, and vegetable. When everyone has finished, remove the popsicles from the freezer. Using the craft stick as a handle, remove the popsicles from the cups. If they are difficult to remove, run a little warm water on the outside of the cup.

While enjoying your supper, see how many rhymes everyone can remember. Let each person tell which nursery rhyme or song is their favorite.

BRER RABBIT'S COUNTRY
NEW YEAR'S EVE SUPPER

Baked Ham glazed with Apricot Sauce
Black-eyed Peas
Tossed Bunny Salad
Steamed Carrots with Ginger
Corn Bread
Iced Tea or Lemonade

My children are big fans of Uncle Remus' stories about the crafty but
dense Brer Fox, his fumbling cohort Brer Bear, and the small but smart Brer
Rabbit. My husband always said he could tell when we were reading a Brer
Rabbit story at bedtime because he'd hear a giggly, raucous chorus
of "Oh, no, Brer Fox. Pleeeeease don't throw me in the briar patch,"
followed by gales of laughter.

The stories are written in a regional Southern accent and are great fun to read
out loud, especially with different voices for each of the characters.
Because the South is represented so strongly by these tall tales, I thought they'd
fit in nicely with some food superstitions tied to the New Year's holiday and,
for me, to the South itself.

If you ask me about the superstition of having black-eyed peas and corn bread
for New Year's, I'd have to tell you what one of my grandmothers told me—every
black-eyed pea you eat on New Year's Day represents one day of good fortune in
the new year, and as for the corn bread, I don't know exactly why eating
corn bread gives you good luck or even if it's true, but we're not
going to risk finding out, just eat.

For Baked Ham, You'll Need:

2 to 3 pound ham
4 large jars apricot baby food
1 cup brown sugar
1 tablespoon spicy mustard
10 whole cloves
1 small can apricot halves

Baking pan or casserole
Mixing bowl
Knife
Spoon
Measuring spoons
Can opener
Measuring cup

Before You Cook:

• Preheat the oven to 350°.

Let's Cook!

Place the ham in the baking dish. Score the top of the ham diagonally with the knife, in one direction, then in the opposite direction so the lines intersect in X's.

In the mixing bowl, combine all of the baby food, brown sugar, and mustard. Open the can of apricots and pour ¼ cup of syrup in the measuring cup (P & K). Add syrup to the mixing bowl (K). Stir the ingredients until they are mixed thoroughly.

Put cloves into the top of the ham where the lines intersect.

Spoon the apricot mixture over the top of the ham and allow it to run down the sides **(P)**.

Put 3 to 4 apricot halves, cut side down, on top of ham **(P & K)**.

Put baking dish into the oven and bake for 1 hour and 15 minutes.

For Steamed Carrots, You'll Need:

1 Package carrots
1 tsp. grated or powdered ginger
Water

Steamer
Peeler
Cutting board
Knife

Before You Cook:

• Wash and pare carrots **(K)**.

Let's Cook!

Cut off tops and tips of carrots **(P)**. Cut carrots into round medallions **(P)**. Put carrots and ginger in the top of the steamer and cover **(K)**.

Fill the bottom of the steamer three-fourths full of water **(P & K)**. Put top of the steamer on and set it on the burner **(P)**. Cook on medium-high setting for approximately 20 minutes or until the carrots are tender.

Use canned black-eyed peas. Open the can and pour contents into a small sauce pan. Cook over a low heat, covered until you are ready to serve the ham **(P & K)**.

Use packaged corn bread mix. Follow package directions. Grease corn muffin pan, and fill each section three-fourths full of batter (P & K). Cook according to package directions.

For Bunny Salad, You'll Need:

1 head of iceberg lettuce
1 package fresh spinach
1 sweet red pepper
1 yellow pepper
1 bunch celery
1 tray of ice cubes
Salad dressing of your choice

Large salad bowl
Sharp knife for cutting
One medium-sized mixing bowl
Cutting bowl

Before You Cook:
• Wash and clean thoroughly all of the vegetables (P & K) and drain.

Let's Cook!
Tear leaves of iceberg lettuce and spinach into salad bowl (P & K). Discard stems from the spinach.

Cut the bottoms off the celery stalks (P) and remove the leaves (K). Use a knife to chop the celery into small pieces (P) and add them to the salad bowl.

Remove the tops of the peppers (P). Use the knife to cut out the center of each pepper and remove all seeds from inside of the pepper (P). Put ice cubes and water into the mixing bowl (P & K). Put the peppers in the bowl for about 5 minutes. Remove peppers from the water and cut into slices (P), then cut into smaller pieces. Add peppers to salad bowl (K).

Use salad tongs to gently toss the ingredients together. Set aside until you are ready to serve.

For Iced Tea, You'll Need:

4 tea bags
1 quart of water
Sugar, to taste
1 tray of ice cubes

Tea kettle
Container for tea (not glass)
Long wooden spoon

Let's Cook!

Boil the water in a tea kettle. Put the tea bags in the serving container.

Pour boiling water over the tea bags (P) and let them steep about 5 minutes. Remove and discard the tea bags (P).

Put ice cubes into the container (K). Fill with cold water (P).

Add the sugar to sweeten to your taste. Use the spoon to stir (P & K)

For Lemonade, You'll Need:

6 large lemons
Water
Sugar to taste

Ice

Blender
Cutting board
Peeler
Knife
Long wooden spoon
Container for serving
Measuring cup

Before You Cook:

• Peel the lemons (P & K).

Let's Cook!

Cut the lemons into halves lengthwise. Remove the seeds. Place the halves in the blender and add ½ cup of water (P & K). Set the blender on the juice setting and run until lemons are completely juiced (P & K).

Add about 4 cups of water to the lemon juice. Put ½ cup of sugar in the blender (P & K). Set the blender on low or mix setting and run until the ingredients are combined (P & K).

Pour the contents of the blender into a container (P). Add ice (K). Fill the container with water (P) and stir (K). If necessary, add sugar to sweeten to your taste.

Slice the ham, serve the salad, and be sure to have at least one helping of black-eyed peas and corn bread for good luck any time of the year.

While enjoying your supper, go around the table and have each person tell what resolutions they made the year before and how many of them they kept. Have each person tell one good thing that happened to them during that year. Have each person tell a story about a funny thing that happened over the past year.

THE WHO-VILLE CHRISTMAS FEAST

Roast Beast
Wiggly Cranberry Sauce
Potato Mountains
Grinch's Green Beans
Who Pudding

I don't know how the holidays go around your house, but at our house
we love every aspect—spiritual, commercial and, of course, the inevitable
television specials. We read *The Night Before Christmas* at bedtime.
Christmas Eve, we go caroling in the neighborhood, we love the sight of holly
sprigs and Christmas wreaths. We also say, "hi," to the jolly guy in the red suit
when we see him, build a Yule log, decorate a tree with ornaments collected
over the past 30 years and take sugar cookies to the firefighters at the station
down the street from us and decorate their outside tree with
special ornaments for the local birds and squirrels.
So you can imagine my children's horror when they found out from Dr. Seuss
that that grand-champion meany, the Grinch, had actually considered stealing
Christmas from the Whos in Who-ville one year. We were certainly happy to
read that the Grinch and his dog, Max, finally learned the meaning of
Christmas and joined the Whos for their traditional feast.
Lest you think my children are little angels,
allow me to say that the only thing my middle daughter thought was
unsatisfactory about Seuss' story was that the Grinch didn't eat Cindy Lou Who
when she interrupted his dastardly work. And you thought
your kids were bloodthirsty...
If your holiday plans call for a family feast, here's the menu from
The Whos Christmas Feast for you to prepare and share.

For Roast Beast, You'll Need:

1 3- to 4-pounds chuck, shoulder, or rump roast

1 teaspoon meat tenderizer

2 tablespoons oil

1 large onion

1 stalk celery

1 bay leaf

Salt and pepper to taste

2 cubes of beef bouillon

Water

Several large leaves of iceberg lettuce

Green seedless grapes

Red seedless grapes

Covered roasting pan

Skillet

Cutting board

Sharp knife for cutting

Measuring cup

Tea kettle

Serving platter or tray

Before You Cook:

- Wash the roast thoroughly and pat dry. Sprinkle on both sides with meat tenderizer. Let sit while preparing the vegetables and stock (P & K).
- Wash the onions and celery (K).
- Preheat the oven to 300°.

Let's Cook!

Put approximately 2 cups of water in a tea kettle and put on a burner at medium high heat to boil (P). Peel the onion and cut into halves, then cut the halves into quarters (P). Put the onion pieces in the roasting pan (K). Cut the leaves, top, and bottom off the celery (P). Chop the celery into small pieces (P) and add the pieces to a roasting pan (K). Unwrap the bouillon cubes and put them in the measuring cup (K). Pour 2 cups of boiling water from tea kettle over the cubes (P). Place the skillet on a burner. Put oil in the skillet and warm on medium-high heat (P). When the skillet is completely heated, sear the meat on all sides (P). Do not scorch it, but make sure it is no longer pink on the outside. Remove the meat from the skillet to a roasting pan (P). Stir the bouillon in the measuring cup (K) then pour over the meat (P). Add the bay leaf to the roasting pan and put the covered roaster in the oven (P & K). Cook for 2 to 3 hours, until the meat is tender and cooked all the way through. During the cooking, turn the meat occasionally, probably about every 30 minutes.

While the roast beast is cooking, prepare potatoes and other dishes.

For Potato Mountains, You'll Need:

5 or 6 medium-sized potatoes

Water

¼ cup milk

⅔ cup butter or margarine

Salt and pepper to taste

Peeler

Large sauce pan

Measuring cup

Spoon

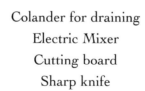

Colander for draining
Electric Mixer
Cutting board
Sharp knife

Before You Cook:

• Wash and peel the potatoes (K).

Let's Cook!

Cut potatoes into 1-inch pieces and place them in the sauce pan (P). Cover the potatoes with water and add about ¼ teaspoon of salt (P & K). Place sauce pan on burner on medium-high heat and bring to an easy boil (P). Let potatoes boil until they are soft when tested with the edge of a spoon. Add water, if necessary, to keep the potatoes from boiling down and scorching (P & K). When potatoes are cooked, pour into a colander in the sink to drain (P). Once drained, return potatoes to the sauce pan (P). Add the butter, milk, and seasonings and stir to combine (P & K). Use an electric mixer on low speed to whip the potatoes until they are fluffy (P & K). Cover the sauce pan and return it to the burner on a low heat until ready to serve.

For Wiggly Cranberry Sauce:

Use canned cranberry sauce. Put can in the refrigerator overnight to chill. When preparing to serve, open both ends of the can and gently push out of the can onto serving plate (P & K). Use a sharp knife to cut the cranberry sauce into ½-inch sections for serving.

For Grinch Green Beans:

Use 1 to 2 cans of green beans. Open can and put green beans in a small sauce pan (K) set on a low heat on the burner (P). If you like, add slivered almonds for a little more exotic taste. Cover the sauce pan and keep on a low heat until ready to serve.

For Who Pudding:

Use 1 or 2 large boxes of instant chocolate pudding and prepare according to the package directions. Pour pudding into plastic champagne glasses and put glasses in refrigerator until ready to serve (P & K).

Just before serving, top each pudding with a dollop of whipped cream and sprinkle lightly with green sugar crystals (P & K). Add a red maraschino cherry on top.

When cooked, remove the roast beast from the oven (P). On serving platter, arrange lettuce leaves and place roast in the center (P). Carve several slices for serving (P), then garnish the platter with grapes (K). Strain some of the pot liquor from the roasting pan through a sieve and serve in a gravy boat as au jus for roast beast and potato mountains.

Over your Who Feast, talk about all of the good, exciting, or fun things you've done during the year. Go around the table and have each person make a Christmas wish for one thing they hope will happen in the next year.

DOUG'S DINNER
(What Mrs. Funnie Serves When Skeeter Spends the Night)

Kids watching television is inevitable in this era of electronic information and entertainment. I don't think that television of itself is necessarily a bad thing, I just despair at the scarcity of quality programming, especially for children. I can't say that my husband and I have always been thrilled by what our children have watched on television, and, in fact, there have been shows we've watched with the kids that we've discussed with them afterward to explain why we were putting the parental kibosh on watching them again.

Like it or not, cartoons are part of children's "literature."

One show that we're particularly fond of is *Doug*.

As my children have gotten older, it was nice to find a show with characters that were a little older, too. And I like the relationships on this show: Doug and his best friend, Skeeter, Doug and his older sister, Judy, and Doug and his friendship for and crush on the delightful Patty Mayonnaise. It's still standard sit-com solve-all-problems-in-30-minutes stuff, but it's a cut above the super hero or talking animals from outer space fare. Here's a simple menu for overnight guests that Mrs. Funnie fixes for Dough and his friends:

Honkerburgers
Bloatsberg Beets
Judy's Dramatic Chocolate Chip Pyramid

For Honkerburgers, You'll Need:

1 to 2 pounds ground beef

1 small onion

1 teaspoon cumin

2 cubes of beef bouillon

1¼ cups water

1 small can tomato paste

1 tablespoon oil

Salt and pepper to taste

1 package hamburger buns

Skillet

Tea kettle

Measuring cup

Wooden spoon

Measuring spoons

Cutting board

Sharp knife

Before You Cook:

- Wash and peel the onion (K).
- Unwrap the bouillon cubes and put them in the measuring cup (K).
- Open the can of tomato paste and set it aside (K).

Let's Cook!

Put water in the tea kettle and heat on medium high heat until boiling (K). Chop the onion into very small pieces (K). Place a skillet on the burner, add oil, and heat on a medium to medium-high heat (P). Break up the ground meat with your hands as you put it in the skillet (P & K). Brown the meat, turning it until none of it is pink (P). Pour 1¼ cups of boiling water into the measuring cup over the bouillon cubes. Stir to dissolve the cubes. Reduce the heat under the beef to low (P). Add the tomato paste, bouillon, and cumin. Stir to combine (P & K). Add salt and pepper to taste (P & K). Simmer, uncovered, until the mixture reduces to the consistency thick enough to stay on a bun without running.

While the Honkerburgers are simmering, prepare the beets.

For Bloatsberg Beets, You'll Need:

1 can of sliced beets
Small sauce pan
Slotted spoon

Before You Cook:
• Open the beets carefully with a can opener (K).

Let's Cook!
Pour the beets into the sauce pan slowly, trying not to "splash." Heat on the burner on low heat until the Honkerburgers are ready (P & K).

For Judy's Dramatic Chocolate Chip Pyramid, You'll Need:

1 10-ounce bag semi-sweet chocolate morsels
1¼ cups flour
½ teaspoon baking soda

¼ teaspoon salt

¾ cup granulated sugar

¾ cup brown sugar

½ cup butter or margarine

2 teaspoons water

2 eggs

1 teaspoon vanilla extract

8-inch square brownie pan

Long wooden spoon

Measuring cup

Measuring spoons

Mixing bowl

Sharp knife

Spatula

Wire rack

Toothpicks

Before You Cook:

- Use a small amount of the oil to grease the brownie pan (P & K).
- Preheat the oven to 325°.

Let's Cook!

Measure the flour, baking soda, and salt into the mixing bowl and set aside (P & K). In the sauce pan, combine the butter, sugars, and water and heat on a burner set on medium to medium-high heat (P & K). Heat the mixture just until it starts to boil, then remove the pan from the heat (P). Stir in chocolate morsels and mix until smooth. Add one egg and stir mixture thoroughly (P & K). Add vanilla and stir well (P & K). Add the flour mixture from the bowl to the chocolate mixture in the sauce pan and stir until all ingredients are moistened and well combined (P & K). Pour the batter into the greased brownie pan. Put the pan in the oven and bake 30 to 40 minutes, until a toothpick inserted into the middle comes out cleanly (P). Remove the pan from the oven and place it on a wire rack to cool. When cooled, cut into 2- to 3-inch squares and remove to a serving plate, stacking them in a pyramid shape using the squares like building blocks (P & K).

After dinner and the cleanup, sit down with the kids to watch their favorite television show or video. Ask which part they like best and why they particularly like this show. After you've listened, tell them what you liked and didn't like about the show and why. Tell them about a television show you really liked when you were the same age they are now. Decide together what you'll watch next. One of the habits I've gotten into on Sundays is getting the local channel guide for the week out of the paper and a highlighter and going through the guide and highlighting the shows I want to make a point of trying to see during the coming week. I also ask my husband about shows that sound like something he would enjoy, and the children, and I go back through the guide to mark the shows they particularly want to watch that week. This is not only a good way to monitor which shows your children like to watch, it's a great opportunity to point them toward shows you'd like them to watch (on The History Channel, Discovery, A&E, PBS, etc. "Didn't you tell me you were working on a report about Alexander the Great? Here's a show we can tape for you so you can get some more information."). The other advantage to this system is that you mediate the remote control disputes *before* the shows come on, saving untold amounts of domestic carnage.

STONE SOUP

One of the first stories I ever remember hearing as a child was *Stone Soup*. I do remember I heard it originally on the *Captain Kangaroo Show*.

Since then, I've probably heard or read a half-dozen variations of the story, originating from several different countries and cultures. I've also theorized that *Stone Soup* may have been one of the things that gave me a life-long love of homemade soups.

In the story, a clever fellow who's starving talks an old lady into sharing her food with him by convincing her that he can make a delicious soup out of nothing but a stone.

Little by little, he gets her to put in a lot of delicious ingredients until they have a terrific pot of soup.

The great thing about Stone Soup is that it contains mainly leftover ingredients from your fridge, and depends entirely on your own tastes. You can use this recipe as a base from which to start, adding and subtracting ingredients you like or already have.

Stone Soup is "built" in at least two stages; you'll prepare a stock, then you'll add fresh vegetables to boil and a little later add ingredients that don't need to cook as long.

You'll Need:

FOR THE STOCK:

1 stone, at least 3 x 3-inch

Small, inexpensive cut of beef or leftover beef, from a roast, steak, etc.

2 Cubes of beef bouillon

Approximately 6 to 8 cups water

FOR THE SOUP:

4 carrots

2 to 3 medium potatoes

2 stalks celery

1 large onion

1 16-ounce can peas

1 16-ounce can green beans

1 16-ounce can whole kernel corn

2 whole bay leaves

1 6-ounce can tomato sauce

2 whole cloves

Salt to taste

Pepper to taste

Optional: any leftover vegetables or canned vegetables you like

Optional: uncooked pasta you like (macaroni, shells, etc.)

Cutting board

Small, sharp knife

Larger knife for cubing beef

Large sauce pan or soup kettle

Measuring cup

Long wooden spoon for stirring

Ladle for serving

Before You Cook:

- If you are using fresh beef, cut it into cubes, and trim off the fat (P), then brown it in a skillet with a teaspoon of vegetable oil until the meat is slightly brown and you don't see any pink or red on the outside of the cubes (P). Set them aside.
- If you are using cooked beef (the leftover pieces from a roast, for example) cut it into cubes and trim off the fat (P).
- If you are using fresh vegetables, peel carrots, potatoes, or onions (K), then cut them into 1-inch cubes or pieces (P), and set them aside.
- If you are using canned vegetables, open the cans (K). Wash your stone thoroughly with mild soap and warm water. Rinse thoroughly (K), otherwise, you'll wind up with Soapy Soup.

Let's Cook!

Pour water into the sauce pan or soup kettle you want to use to combine all the ingredients and cook the soup in (K). Set the burner on medium-high heat and add approximately ½ teaspoon of salt to the water (P & K). Bring water to a rolling boil. Add bouillon cubes to the water and stir until they dissolve (P & K). Add cubed meat and lower the heat slightly (P). Boil the meat for about 30 minutes. Add water if the stock boils down (P & K). Add fresh vegetables to the stock and enough water to cover them. Put in the bay leaves, cloves, salt, pepper, and tomato sauce (P & K). Stir the ingredients occasionally and let them cook until the vegetables are soft when cut with the side of a spoon (P). When fresh vegetables are cooked, add the canned and leftover vegetables and optional ingredients (P & K). Lower the heat, correct the seasonings, and simmer about 20 minutes. Remove and throw away bay leaves and cloves. Use the ladle to serve in bowls or cups.

FAMILY SAFETY TIP: Clove oil or handling whole cloves may cause dermatitis or an allergic reaction in some people. I suggest everyone wash their hands after handling any herbs or seasonings they don't come in contact with very often.

Sharing the story of *Stone Soup* over a bowl of your own creation is a great rainy, cold, or snowy day activity. Next time you're at the library, see how many different versions you can find and how many cultures and historical eras they represent.

THE OWL AND THE PUSSYCAT'S ISLAND LUAU

One of the most well-travelled couples in fairy tales is the *Owl and the Pussycat,* who prefer sea cruises to more modern transportation. Ever since Edward Lear brought them to life in his poem, they've sailed through many children's lives in their beautiful green boat.

Being adventurous tourists, they've sampled exotic cuisines from their many ports of call, but their favorite is the island luau thrown in their honor after they were married by the turkey who lived on the hill. It's reasonable to expect that after all that mince and all those slices of quince, they were ready for a culinary change.

You can sample their island luau either inside your house or, if you've got room to safely build a fire pit outside, you can try your hand at cooking island-style on the next tropical day where you live.

Luau Mini-Meat Loaves
Tropical Fruit Tree
Banana Boats

If you're cooking inside:

For Luau Mini-Meat Loaves, You'll Need:

1 pound hamburger

1 egg

½ teaspoon salt

¼ teaspoon pepper

1 packet dried onion soup mix

6 saltine crackers

8 to 10 cabbage leaves

4 slices Cheddar or Swiss cheese

1 tablespoon water

Foil

Large mixing bowl

Cutting board

Measuring spoons

Colander

Before You Cook:

- Preheat the oven to 400°.
- Wash and drain the cabbage leaves in the colander **(K)**.
- Tear off four squares of aluminum foil about 12 inches square **(P & K)**.

Let's Cook!

In the mixing bowl, break up the hamburger **(K)**. Crumble the crackers, two at a time, crushing them with your hands over the meat in the bowl **(K)**. Add salt and pepper and onion soup mix **(P & K)**. Break the egg into the bowl (P & K) and discard the shells. Using clean hands, mish the ingredients together until all have been completely combined (P & K).

Make 8 to 10 balls out of the hamburger mixture (P & K). Put half the hamburger balls on the cutting board and use your palms to flatten the balls slightly (P & K). Put one slice of cheese on top of each portion of hamburger (K). Put another hamburger ball on top of each of the first hamburger portion (P & K) and flatten the top portion (P & K). Form each of the hamburger portions into a loaf shape (P & K). Put one large cabbage leaf or two smaller leaves overlapping each other on the board and sit one meat loaf in the center of the leaf (P & K). Roll the cabbage leaf around the loaf and place it on a square of aluminum foil (P & K). Form a packet around the loaf and roll the top and sides down to seal it (P & K). Repeat the process with all of the hamburger until you have four packets. Place the packets on the lowest rack of the oven (P) and reduce the temperature to 350°. Bake approximately 30 minutes.

While the luau loaves cook, prepare the fruit tree and banana boats.

For Tropical Fruit Tree, You'll Need:

Large pineapple
Cantaloupe
Honeydew
Apple
Small Strawberries

Sharp knife for cutting
Peeler
Colander
Toothpicks
Cutting board

Before You Cook:

- Wash and drain all the fruit (K)
- Peel and core the apple (P & K).
- Cut the cantaloupe and honeydew melons in half (P). Use the spoon to scrape out all the seeds and discard them (K).
- Cut the tops off of the strawberries (P).
- Cut the apple in half, then into cubes (P) and set them aside. Cut the melon halves into crescent-shaped slices, about 2" wide at the rind (P). Use the knife to cut the melon off of the rind and cut it into rough 1-inch cubes (P). Set aside.
- Cut the base off of the pineapple (P). Stand the pineapple upright on a serving plate or platter.
- Stick one end of a toothpick into a piece of fruit and then stick the exposed end into the pineapple (P & K). Alternate the pieces around the pineapple, starting at the base, for example: cantaloupe, apple, strawberry, honeydew (P & K). Stop when you reach the top of the pineapple, leaving the pineapple's leaves as the very top.

For Banana Boats, You'll Need:

1 Large banana per person
Small bag semi-sweet chocolate morsels
Small bag of marshmallows (colored ones, if you can find them)

Sharp knife
Cutting board
Aluminum foil

Before You Cook:

• Leave the oven set at 350°.

• Tear off pieces of foil about 6 inches long, one for each banana.

Let's Cook!

Use the knife to cut out a wedge down the length of the banana (P). Lift off the wedge, save the peel. In the cut-out, sprinkle morsels and marshmallow (P & K). Replace the peel over them (K) and wrap the banana in one piece of aluminum foil (P & K). Remove the meat loaf packets from the oven (P). Unwrap the packets and put them on plates (P & K). Use the fruit tree as a centerpiece for the table and let everyone "pick" their favorite fruits off of the "tree" to eat. Two minutes before you are finished, put the banana boats in the oven (P). After 2 minutes, remove the packets from the oven, fold down the foil around the banana, and remove the top peel. Use a spoon to scoop out bites of banana, chocolate and marshmallow.

If you plan to cook outside: Prepare the foods as described above.

To build the fire pit for the luau: Find a flat, dry piece of ground as far away from trees and bushes as you can get. Have a bucket of sand or water next to the pit just in case and gather enough large stones (or bricks if you're in your backyard) to line the pit and surround the rim at ground level. Use a shovel to loosen the top layer of grass or plants (2 to 6 inches deep) where you plan to dig the pit. Carefully shovel the top layer to one side away from the pit so you can replace it when you are finished. The pit doesn't have to be big—about 3 feet in diameter and about 2 feet deep should be enough—and you'll need the dirt you remove later, so put it in a pile near the pit.

Gather tinder, kindling, and firewood and build a "teepee" fire at the bottom of the pit. Tinder is the small, fast-burning fuel you use to start the fire; kindling are small branches or pieces that catch and make the body of the fire; and the firewood is the larger logs that will burn the longest once they start. For this kind of fire, you'll need mainly kindling, because it does not have to burn as long or as hot as a large, open cooking fire. Once you get the fire started by lighting the tinder and the kindling begins to burn, add 1 or 2 larger pieces of kindling or firewood so you will have coals as the fire burns down. Line the pit with stones and place some on top of the coals being careful to leave some space between them so the fire can "breathe."

Depending on the dampness of the ground and the dryness and sizes of your wood, this process will probably take about 30 minutes to 1 hour. If you want to speed up the process, instead of wood, you can use charcoal at the bottom of the pit and light it safely as you would any cooking fire in a barbecue grill.

Wrap the mini-meat loaves in aluminum foil and place them on the cooking stones at the bottom of the pit. You can leave the packets uncovered while you cook them about half an hour then use long tongs to turn them over and cook them 30 more minutes. You can also cover the packets with a layer of large green (fresh) leaves (palm fronds, for example) or you can cover the packets with a layer of small stones to help them cook evenly.

There are a lot of variables in outdoor cooking, so you have to play it by ear and use a large dose of common sense. The best way to judge cooking time is to remove one of the packets with long tongs, unwrap the packet and make a cut into the middle of the loaf and check to make sure that the meat has cooked thoroughly all the way through. Always err on the side of caution—with the meat wrapped in the cabbage leaves you can afford to cook it a little longer. If the fire or weather are not cooperative, cook the packets in the oven as in the directions for indoor cooking.

The Banana Boats can be prepared in the pit, too, and are only left on the stones long enough to melt the marshmallows.

SAFETY TIP: If you are cooking with the fire pit, do not leave the open fire or the lined cooking pit unattended. When you have finished your luau, use the shovel to move the cooking stones off of the coals, break the coals up and pour your sand or water over them. Wait a few minutes to make sure you have doused or drowned them. After letting the pit cool, remove the stones, make sure the coals are out, then shovel the dirt you removed from the pit back into it. Carefully replace the top layer of sod or soil over the pit and gently use your shoed feet to tamp it down. Put the stones, rocks, or bricks back where you found them.

For a wonderful, whimsical version of this old favorite, find Lear's *The Owl and the Pussycat* illustrated by Jan Brett. Her art work is imaginative and colorful and adds a lot of dimension to this simple poem. My family especially liked the relationship between the Pussycat's pet fish and the fish who has followed the boat. You can use this story-poem to encourage your family to write a poem about your family's last or favorite vacation and draw pictures to go along with it. You can also use the same idea to help pre-readers learn words through visual connections. We took pictures of our trip to the zoo (children and animals), then put them in a photo album labeled in printed words on index cards underneath each picture. This helped them connect written words with the thing they represent, and as they developed, helped cue them when sounding out words because they already knew the names of the animals in the pictures.

MAX'S WILD DINNER

How fantastic would dinner have to be to make you give up the title of "King"
and come back from the place Where the Wild Things Are?

Pretty fantastic!

I first read Maurice Sendak in a (literally) tiny collection of little red
books called "The Nutshell Library," put together in its own box with Sendak
illustrations on the outside. I bought it myself in a little shop in Tyler, Texas,
one long, hot summer day while I was visiting my grandmother, who ran the
shoe store a couple of doors down from this shop. I occupied some of my time that
summer delighting in these quick pieces of poetry and prose. I loved *Chicken
Soup with Rice* and the one about Pierre (who didn't care).

When I went back to school that fall and started the second grade, I was thrilled
to discover Sendak's *Where the Wild Things Are* in my school library. My
favorite part of *Wild Things* has always been Max's "monster" suit
because I thought it made him look like a menacing bunny while he cavorted
with the monsters before returning home.

Now if you travel with me about twenty years forward
and hundreds of miles from that first shop, I was looking for gifts for
my eldest daughter for her fifth birthday. While I was browsing through a small
shop for gift wrap and gift tags and odds and ends for the upcoming event,
I stumbled upon something that really surprised me. There, on one of the back
shelves labeled "Gift Books," was a little box with Maurice Sendak illustrations
on it containing four tiny red books and labeled "The Nutshell Library."

I bought it, of course, to give to my daughter.

The real thrill in all of this for me was not just rediscovering a favorite
collection from my childhood, or even passing it on to my child, but sitting
down together to enjoy these little books and seeing the animation and delight
on her face as she would begin jumping in with the ends of the lines. Sharing
the great loves of our own childhood reading and seeing that love take root in

our children to carry into the future with them to others is so exciting
that it's almost impossible to describe.
At the end of *Where the Wild Things Are*, Max, the little boy in the story,
returns to his room to find his supper on a tray for him. You and your
"wild things" may enjoy making Max's supper together
after a tough day of cavorting.

Chicken Soup with Rice
Exotic Jungle Birds
Overgrown Greens
Vegetation
Back Home Brownies

For Chicken Soup with Rice, You'll Need:

1 can chicken with rice Soup

or

Leftover cooked chicken

8 cups chicken stock (or 8 cups water and 2 cubes of chicken bouillon)

1 cup rice

2 carrots

Salt and pepper to taste

Small onion

Parsley flakes

Small saucepan

Stirring spoon

Ladle

Saucepan with a cover

Measuring cup

Sharp knife

Peeler

Can opener

Cutting board

Measuring spoons

If you are using canned soup: Open the soup with the can opener and use the small saucepan to prepare the soup according to the directions on the label (P & K). Simmer on a low heat while you prepare the rest of the meal.

If you are making the soup yourself:

Before You Cook:

- Use the peeler to clean the carrots (K). Wash them then cut the ends and tips off (P).
- Dice the carrots into very small pieces (P). Put them aside.
- If you are using leftover chicken, pull it off the bones (P & K). Cut the chicken into very small pieces. Set aside.
- You'll need about ¼ cup of onions, so wash and peel a small onion. Dice the onion until you have the necessary amount. Set aside.

Let's Cook!

(If you are using chicken stock, skip the preparation of the stock.)

Put 2 cups of water in the saucepan (P & K) along with a dash of salt, and put the pan on a medium-high heat until it begins to boil. Unwrap bouillon cube (K) and drop it into the boiling water. Stir until the cube dissolves (P & K). Pour the rice into the water, stir, cover, and immediately lower the heat to low heat (P & K). Do not uncover the saucepan for about 25 minutes.

While the rice is cooking, put the other 6 cups of water into another saucepan and set it on a medium high heat until it boils (P & K). When it boils, unwrap the other bouillon cube (K) and drop it into the boiling water (P). Stir until the cube dissolves (P & K). Add the chicken, onion, and carrots to the stock (P & K). Cover and lower heat to medium until mixture stays on a low boil. Boil until rice is ready.

Uncover the rice (P) and add it to the boiling stock (P). Season lightly with salt and pepper (P & K) and add about 1 tablespoon of parsley flakes (P & K). Stir briefly then cover again and bring it back to a low boil for about 30 minutes or until the carrots are thoroughly cooked. Set the heat on a low setting and simmer until you are ready to serve it. Add additional water if the soup begins to reduce, then adjust the seasonings again. Stir occasionally (P & K).

For Exotic Jungle Birds, You'll Need:

1 Cornish game hen for each person

1 cup ketchup

¼ cup brown sugar

2 tablespoons lemon juice

2 to 3 onions

1 tablespoon Worcestershire sauce

Large bunch of green onions (whole chives)

1 tablespoon mustard

Large casserole or deep baking pan with a 2- to 3-inch lip, large enough to get a wire rack in the bottom of the pan

Bowl

Pastry brush

Measuring cup

Measuring spoons

Sharp knife

Mixing spoon

Aluminum foil

Before You Cook:

- Preheat the oven to 450°.
- Thoroughly, inside and out, wash the game hens **(P)**. Pull out any gizzards, etc., left inside body cavity and discard **(P)**. Pat dry and set aside.
- Wash the chives and drain them **(K)**. Cut off the tips of the greens and the bottom of the white bulbs and discard trimmings **(P)**. Set the onions aside.

- If you are using a fresh lemon instead of bottled lemon juice, cut the lemon in half (P), remove the seeds, and squeeze the juice into a small bowl and set it aside (P & K).
- Wash and peel the onions (K). Cut each onion into halves and quarters (P). Set the pieces aside.

Let's Cook!

Rub each hen with a little salt (approximately ⅛ teaspoon) on the outside (P & K). Put 1 or 2 pieces of onion inside each bird (K). Place the hens on the rack at the bottom of the casserole or baking pan (you can use more than one casserole if you need to and place them on separate racks inside the oven) (P & K). Place the hens in the oven and immediately lower the heat to 350°. Roast the birds about 45 minutes. When the hens are put in the oven, prepare the basting sauce.

In a mixing bowl, combine the ketchup, brown sugar, lemon juice, Worcestershire sauce, and mustard (P & K). Whisk ingredients together until completely blended (P & K). After the birds have roasted about 30 minutes, use pastry brush to "paint" sauce all over the tops of the birds. Return them to the oven for 15 minutes.

Prepare the dinner plates for serving by fanning 3 or 4 of the green onions out on each plate. Baste the birds with the sauce once again and cook for another 15 minutes. The hens are cooked when you make a small cut with a sharp knife in the meaty part of the leg (drumstick) and the juices run clear. When cooked, remove birds from the oven (P). Place one hen on each plate, with the bird laying on the bed of greens make by the onions.

For Overgrown Greens, You'll Need:

1 head red-tipped Romaine lettuce

1 large bunch fresh spinach

1 small head red cabbage

1 small bunch radishes

1 cucumber

2 carrots

1 yellow pepper (if you can find one)

Your favorite salad dressing

Cutting board

Colander

Sharp knife

Big bowl for serving

2 serving forks

Grater

Peeler

Plastic Wrap

Before You Cook:

- Wash and drain in the colander all of the greens and vegetables (K).
- Pull the leaves off of the head of lettuce, tearing them into smaller pieces and placing them in the salad bowl (K). Pull the stems off of the spinach leaves; tear the leaves and put them in the salad bowl. Use a sharp knife to cut very thin sections off the red cabbage (P); tear these into smaller pieces and add them to the salad bowl (K). Use the peeler to scrape the carrots; cut the tips and ends off the carrots and discard them (P). Add

the carrots to the salad bowl.

- Cut off both ends of the cucumber (P). Cut the cucumber into thin slices (P) and put the slices into the salad bowl.

- Cut the tips and ends off of the radishes (P) and discard them. Cut the radishes in halves across the width (P) and add them to the salad bowl.

- Remove the top of the pepper (P) and use either the knife (P) or a spoon (K) to take out the pepper's core and scrape out all the seeds. Cut the pepper in half lengthwise (P), then cut the pepper into very thin strips (P) and add these to the bowl, too.

- Using the salad tongs or serving forks, lightly toss the ingredients of the salad together (P & K). Put plastic wrap over the bowl and refrigerate it until you're ready to serve.

For Vegetation, You'll Need:

Canned, whole asparagus spears

or

One bunch of fresh asparagus

Water

Saucepan

Steamer

Sharp knife

Slotted spoon for serving

Can opener

Fork

If you are using canned asparagus: Open the can with the can opener (P & K) and discard the lid (P). Pour contents, including liquid, into saucepan (K). Cover and set on low heat while you are preparing other dishes.

If you are using fresh asparagus:

Before You Cook:

- Wash and drain the asparagus (K). Use the knife to trim off some of the white ends (P) and discard them.
- Put 2 to 4 cups of water in the bottom of the steamer (P & K) and put the asparagus spears in the top of the steamer (P & K).
- Set the steamer on a medium-high heat and let spears steam approximately 20 to 30 minutes or until the spears are tender when poked with a fork (P). While they are cooking, be sure to check the water in the steamer occasionally and add more water if needed (P).

For Back Home Brownies, You'll Need:

4 squares unsweetened baking chocolate

¾ cup butter or margarine

1¾ cups sugar

3 eggs

1 teaspoon vanilla extract

1½ cups all-purpose flour

½ cup milk

Oil

9-inch square pan

Saucepan

Mixing bowl

Wooden spoon for stirring

Measuring cup

Measuring spoons

Toothpicks

Knife

Before You Cook:

• Use the oil to grease the 9-inch pan (K).

• Preheat the oven to 325°.

Let's Cook!

Put the chocolate squares and butter in the saucepan (P & K) and set on a
very low heat. Stir constantly (K) until the ingredients have melted, but do
not cook them any more than that. In the mixing bowl combine the sugar,
eggs, and vanilla (P & K). Add the melted chocolate mixture to the bowl
(P). Stir in the milk (P & K) and combine all the ingredients. Add flour to
the mixing bowl and stir until all the ingredients are thoroughly blended
and smooth Pour the mixture into the greased pan (P & K) and spread
evenly with the back of the spoon. Place the pan in the oven and bake for
30 to 40 minutes.

Use the toothpicks to check for doneness by inserting one into the center of the pan and removing it (P & K). When the toothpick comes out not
moist but with crumbs on it, the brownies are ready.

Remove the pan from the oven (P) and let the pan cool. Cut the brownies into squares with the knife (P). I suggest you make these either before
dinner and let them cool or after dinner so they can bake while everyone is
helping with the cleanup in the kitchen.

While you're eating brownies, be sure to read *Where the Wild Things Are*
or your favorite Maurice Sendak story. You can make a drawing of your
favorite monsters or, if you have some paper plates, use them to make monster masks out of odds and ends like yarn, buttons, and even uncooked
pasta like macaroni or bow tie pasta.

CLOUDY WITH A CHANCE
OF MEATBALLS

Sometimes, reading solves a mystery. Sometimes, reading leads you to another mystery. That is what happened to me when someone told me about *Cloudy with a Chance of Meatballs* by Judi Barrett.

In the story, the reader learns about a place called Chewandswallow where the natives never have to shop for food because things like pancakes and syrup rain on the town. The people have everything from mashed potatoes to hot dogs fall on their fair city. Trouble sets in when the weather goes haywire and giant pieces of toast sail out of the sky and buildings are smashed by huge meatballs that fall like hail on Chewandswallow.

The people of Chewandswallow sail across the sea and find a new place to live and eventually get used to the idea of grocery shopping, cooking food, and using refrigerators.

But when I read *Cloudy with a Chance of Meatballs*, I wondered "Who are the people of Chewandswallow and where did they go?"

My children and I had read about a group of people with a suspiciously similar history. We think the people of Chewandswallow may be Wends.

What's a Wend?

We discovered at the big annual party at the Institute of Texan Cultures in San Antonio that the Wends were a group of about 500 people who left Lusatia (part of what was once Prussia) and took a sailing vessel called *The Ben Nevis* from Liverpool, England, to Texas in the 1800s. Serbin, Texas, is, as far as I know, the only place in the world where Wendish is still spoken today. The Wends are good at several things—quilting, wine-making, blacksmithing, and sausage stuffing—but they are particularly famous for one thing: Wendish noodles. Every year in Giddings, Texas, there is a Wendish Fest and the highlight of the activities is the State of Texas Noodle Cook-off.

A Wendish lady that we met at the Institute of Texan Cultures was nice enough to teach all of us how to make homemade Wendish noodles so we could enjoy them at home. As soon as I read *Cloudy with a Chance of Meatballs*, I began piecing things together until now I am nearly convinced that the people who left Chewandswallow were, in fact, Wends, and that *Witajcze K'nam* may actually mean "We're from Chewandswallow."

Chewandswallow Meatballs
Wendish Noodles
Simply Great Crunchy Cake

For Meatballs, You'll Need:

1 pound hamburger
1 egg
6 saltine crackers
1 small onion
¼ cup ketchup
½ teaspoon Worcestershire sauce
⅛ teaspoon nutmeg
1 package brown gravy mix (powdered)
Oil

Heavy skillet
Sharp knife
Mixing bowl
Cutting board

Measuring spoons
Plate
Wire rack
Paper towels
Metal slotted spoon

Before You Cook:

- Wash and peel the onion (K). Dice the onion and set aside (P).
- Put several paper towels on the counter near the stove and set the wire rack on it (K).

Let's Cook!

In the mixing bowl break up the hamburger with your clean hands (K). Crush the crackers two at a time over the bowl and add them to the hamburger (K). Add the onion, ketchup, Worcestershire sauce, nutmeg, and gravy mix (P & K). Crack the egg into the bowl and discard the shells (P & K).

With your hands, mash the ingredients together until all of them are completely and thoroughly mixed (P & K).

Break the hamburger mix into small pieces about the size of a ping-pong ball and roll each one in your palms to form a small ball (P & K).

Put the skillet on a burner set on medium to medium-high heat with 2 tablespoons of oil (P). When the oil is hot, carefully place the meatballs in the skillet (P). Do not drop them in so they "splash" the hot oil. When one side of the meatball has browned, roll it with the slotted spoon so it rests on a different side (P & K). Repeat on all sides until the whole meatball is browned, usually 6 to 8 minutes.

Remove each browned meatball from the skillet with the slotted spoon and place it on the rack over the paper towels to drain (P).

Continue browning the meatballs until you have used all of the hamburger mix **(P & K).** Put the meatballs on a plate and set in a warm oven (about 150°) until the noodles are ready.

For Wendish Noodles, You'll Need:

3 eggs

2 tablespoons water

¼ teaspoon salt

2½ cups flour

4 cups water

4 beef bouillon cubes

Small bunch of fresh parsley or 2 tablespoons parsley flakes

3 green onions

⅛ teaspoon nutmeg

1 tablespoon butter or margarine

Measuring cup

Measuring spoons

Large mixing bowl

Cutting board

Small sharp knife

Rolling pin

Large spoons for mixing

Colander for draining noodles

Large saucepan

Large serving bowl

Large plate or platter

Long wooden spoon

Before You Cook:

- Wash and drain the parsley (if you are using fresh parsley) and the green onions (K).
- Chop the parsley (P) and the tops of the green onions (P) and set aside.

Let's Cook!

In the mixing bowl, break the eggs (P & K) and discard the shells. Add 2 tablespoons of water and the salt, and beat the ingredients together (P & K). Add about 2½ cups of flour and thoroughly stir all of the ingredients until they form a stiff dough (P & K). Let the dough rest about 15 minutes.

Divide the dough into five balls (P & K). Use one ball of dough at a time, leaving the unused balls in the mixing bowl, covered with a clean dish towel while you are working with one ball. Dust the cutting board lightly with flour and flour your hands and the rolling pin (P & K). Roll out the dough about ¼-inch thick, making it roughly rectangular (P & K). Let the dough dry 5 to 10 minutes. The drier it is when you cut it, the less likely the noodles are to stick together.

Use the small, sharp knife to cut the dough into strips about 2 inches wide (P). Then cut them into lengths about 8 to 10 inches long (P). Stack them on the platter or plate (P & K). Repeat the process until you have used all five balls of dough (P & K). If the balls begin to dry before you are ready to use them, wet the dish towel and wring it out until it is almost dry, then recover the bowl. That should help keep the dough moist until you are ready for it.

Put the saucepan with 4 cups of water in it on a burner set on a medium-high heat (P). When the water boils, unwrap the bouillon cubes and carefully put them in the water (P & K). Stir with the long, wooden spoon until the cubes dissolve (K). Put 3 cups of your noodles into the boiling stock (P & K). Add the butter to the stock (P) and stir with the long, wooden spoon

(K). Let the noodles cook about 10 minutes but do not over-boil or they'll become mushy. Add about half of the green onions, parsley, and nutmeg to the noodles (P & K) and stir. Carry the pan to the sink (P) and remove the noodles from the pan to the colander and let them drain thoroughly (P). Return the pan with the stock in it to the burner (P) and add more noodles (P & K). Repeat the same steps above and pour the drained noodles from the colander to your serving bowl (P). The bowl can be set in a warm oven (about 150°) until the rest of the noodles have been prepared.

Add water about ½ cups at a time if necessary and add the remainder of the onions, parsley, and nutmeg (P & K).

When all the noodles have been cooked, serve them along with your Chewandswallow Meatballs.

You may want to prepare your Simply Great Crunchy Cake before supper so it will be ready for dessert when you are.

For Simply Great Crunchy Cake, You'll Need:

¼ cup and 3 tablespoons butter or margarine

1 cup sugar

1½ cups flour

2 teaspoons baking powder

½ teaspoon salt

1 egg

⅔ cups milk

2 teaspoons cinnamon

1½ cups unfrosted corn flakes

2 medium-sized mixing bowls

Measuring cups

Measuring spoons

Mixing spoons

1 8-inch square baking pan

Sharp knife

Serving plates

Small saucepan

Before You Cook:

• Preheat the oven to 425°.

• Use the oil (about 1 tablespoon) to grease the bottom and sides of the baking pan (K).

Let's Cook!

In one bowl combine the flour, baking powder and salt (P & K). Add ⅓ cup of sugar and beat the mixture until it becomes slightly fluffy (P & K). Break the egg over the bowl (P & K) and discard the shell. Beat all of the ingredients together, then add the milk (P & K). Put the dry ingredients from the first bowl into the bowl with the wet ingredients (P & K), and stir just until you have blended the ingredients together without beating them (P & K).

Wash and dry the first bowl (P & K). Pour the batter into the greased baking pan (P & K). In the saucepan melt the remaining ¼ cup of butter (P & K) over a very low heat. When it has melted, remove the pan from stove (P). Pour the butter into the clean mixing bowl (P). Add ⅔ cup of sugar (K) and the cinnamon (P & K) and mix thoroughly (P & K). Gently fold in the corn flakes (P & K) by using the mixing spoon to move the mixture from the bottom and sides of the bowl over the top of the corn flakes, repeating the motion until all the ingredients are combined, but crunching the corn flakes as little as possible. Use the spoons to spread the mixture over the top of the batter in the baking pan (P & K). Put the baking pan in the oven (P) and bake about 25 minutes. You can test for doneness by inserting the toothpicks into the center of the cake (P & K). The cake is ready when no crumbs or moisture stick to the toothpick.

Remove the baking pan from the oven. Use the sharp knife to cut the cake into squares (P). You can serve this tasty cake either hot or cold.

While you're enjoying your homemade noodles, talk abut where your family's ancestors came from. Did they take a boat like the people leaving Chewandswallow or the Wends leaving Prussia, or did they migrate from South America to North America? If you don't know where they came from, try looking in the genealogical section of your local library for hints about your family's name, or better yet, try my favorite reference—living history books, otherwise known as grandparents or great-grandparents. They are an amazing resource for information on day-to-day living during great periods of history (what kinds of foods did your grandparents eat during the Depression?) and can probably fill you in on family names and what part of this country your family comes from, as well as give you an idea of where to begin your hunt for your ancestors. And if you'd like more information about the Wends, write to the Wendish Heritage Society at Route 2, Box 155, Giddings, Texas 78942-9769. Who knows...your family's name could be Wendish, too!

Smacky Snacks

A neglected category of food in almost everyone's house is snacks. Everyone eats them, after school or work, watching television or just as something quick to nibble on between meals, but we all seem to pretend they don't exist. So, instead of shopping for and preparing fun or nutritious snacks, we go for the easy—and high calorie—fix, like a bag potato chips or store-bought cookies.

As I've mentioned before, I have nothing against saving time and there are times when the convenience foods on the fly are actually the best solution. But I'm even more in favor of anything that gives us a chance to be in the kitchen together, especially when the end-product is something tasty to munch on.

So I've included this section for snacks ranging from quick, nutritious milkshakes, to snacks that will keep kids occupied for a whole afternoon, to t.v. munchies the whole family can enjoy while relaxing in the evening.

If you think snacks can't be "memorable" foods, think of how many times, as an adult, you've heard people speak fondly of the special treat a favorite aunt or uncle or grandparent always brought on each visit, or about their memories of making popcorn balls with siblings on weekend nights when they were just "hanging around."

My own favorite snack is slightly bizarre, but absolutely wonderful. During the summer I spent with my favorite aunt, my mother's youngest sister, and her family, my aunt Zoe and I fell into a habit late Friday nights. I was occupying the finished basement of their house, which was used as a family rec room and alternate t.v. room *cum* den and was also where Aunt Zoe did her laundry and ironing. We discovered that one of the things we had in common was a love of scary black and white movies and old t.v. shows. Every Friday, after everyone else was settled into their beds for the night, the two of us would meet in the kitchen in our pajamas, giggling like little kids, to prepare a snack for watching our "guilty pleasures" shows on the basement television so we wouldn't wake the rest of the household.

After several trial runs, we finally hit on the ideal snack—Garlic Cheerios and ice cold root beer. We'd melt butter in a saucepan, stir in an ample amount of toasted oats and season them with a healthy dose of garlic salt. I know...it still sounds weird...but as one of my own daughters discovered much later, it goes perfectly with root beer, *Alfred Hitchcock Presents, The Outer Limits,* ironing, playing with each other's hair, and teenage angst.

After you've tried these Smacky Snacks, share your own personal favorites, no matter how weird, with your family.

THE BIG BAD WOLF'S FAVORITE T.V. SNACK

Pigs in a Blanket

First of all, let me say that that famous huffing and puffing episode
was an awfully long time ago. Since then, the wolf has moved out of the forest,
settled in a nice neighborhood in a rather large city and, last I heard,
was successfully selling homeowners' insurance.
This recipe is good for a snack while watching television in the evenings,
at a slumber party, or as a fast portable lunch or supper for times when everyone
needs to be somewhere else. And, of course, it's a tasty and socially acceptable
substitute for snacking on your neighbors.

You'll Need:

2 packages biscuits (enough to make 20 biscuits)
2 packages hot dogs (20)
Flour
10 slices processed cheese or 20 small slices mild cheddar
Optional: Salad mustard

Spatula
Baking sheets
Aluminum foil
Small bowl
Cutting board
Sharp knife
Rolling pin
Toothpicks
Knife for spreading

Before You Cook:

- Preheat the oven to 425°.
- If you are using wrapped slices of processed cheese, unwrap them **(K)**, and divide or cut them in half **(P)**. Put them on a plate until you are ready for them. Discard the plastic wrappers. If you are cutting slices of cheddar from a block of cheese, **(P)** does the cutting and **(K)** puts the slices on a plate to use later.
- Dust the cutting board lightly with flour. Put a little flour in your hand and use it to dust the rolling pin until most of its surface is covered **(K)**. Fill the small bowl with water and put it near the cutting board.

Let's Cook!

Open one package of biscuits and one package of hot dogs. Put one biscuit on the cutting board and use the rolling pin to roll the biscuit out flatter (P & K). If you want a spicier snack, spread mustard lightly on the biscuit. Place one slice of cheese on the biscuit (P). Put the hot dog on top of the cheese. Starting at the top of the biscuit, the side farthest from you, roll the biscuit and cheese around the hot dog until you are about ½-inch from the edge closest to you (P & K). Wet your fingertips in the small bowl of water and dab water along the edge of the biscuit (P & K). Continue rolling up the hot dog and seal by pressing down on the damp edge. To make it more secure you can put a toothpick through the whole roll-up. Place the wrapped "piggie" on the baking sheet (P & K). Repeat the steps above until you have used all the ingredients. Put the baking sheet in the oven for 9 to 12 minutes, or until the biscuits are golden brown.

Remove the sheet from the oven and use the spatula to put the piggies in a serving basket or on a plate or platter (P). Let them cool for just a few minutes, then dig in.

Depending on age and appetite, this recipe generally serves six small people or four larger ones.

AN ALADDIN SNACK
FOR ONE ARABIAN NIGHT

(Best when prepared to the music of "Sheherazade")

When my two eldest daughters were two and three, we lived
in a very small town in Texas. My husband, a theatrical rigger, was helping to
restore a theater in Boulder, Colorado, and was often away from home for as
long as eight weeks at a time. You can probably imagine how stimulating the
conversation was around my house at the time, but when I was beginning to
think what a good-looking a guy Fred Rogers was, I knew it was time
to exercise my brain a little.

I put my portable tape player in the kitchen and dug up all the
classical and instrumental music I could find. As I cooked, I told my squirmy
daughters to close their eyes and listen to the music, so they could "see" the story
of the music in their minds. Over lunch or dinner they would ask me to play the
music again so they could tell me their stories. Then they would want to hear
my story about the same music.

My personal favorite has always been "Sheherazade."
It's very "story" music and, naturally, it makes you think of exotic Persian fairy
tales like Aladdin and the Magic Lamp, Ali Baba and the Forty Thieves and the
tales from the thousand and one Arabian nights. In addition to the
written stories about genies, flying carpets, and magical events,
you can always make up your own stories.
Here's a menu for a snack for one Arabian night your family
can have some fun with:

Aladdin's Date Nut Bread
Orange Slices

You'll Need:

1 orange per person

3 cups flour

¾ cup granulated sugar

¾ cup brown sugar

1 teaspoon salt

1 cup pitted dates

¼ teaspoon allspice

2 tablespoons butter or margarine

2 teaspoons baking soda

1 egg

2 teaspoons baking powder

1 cup shelled pecans (or nuts of your choice)

2 teaspoons vanilla extract

2 cups water

An empty one-pound coffee can, cleaned and dried

Vegetable oil

Large mixing bowl

Measuring cup

Measuring spoons

Spoon for mixing

Cutting board

Sharp knife for cutting

Kettle or sauce pan for boiling water

Whisk

Small bowl

Baking sheet

Before You Cook:

- Preheat oven to 350°.
- Wash the oranges (K). Cut them into quarters or eighths (P) and put them on a plate. Store the oranges in the refrigerator until the rest of the snack is ready.
- Chop the dates and nuts into small pieces (P). Set them aside.
- Use the vegetable oil to grease the inside of the clean, empty coffee can. Flour the coffee can very lightly (P & K).
- Break the egg into the small bowl and throw away the shell (P & K). Use the whisk to beat the egg lightly.

Let's Cook!

Put the water in the tea kettle and put on the burner at a medium-high heat until it boils. Combine the sugar, dates, salt, butter, allspice and baking soda in the mixing bowl (P & K). Pour in the boiling water (P). Stir these ingredients together and let sit until cool.

Add the egg and vanilla to the cool mixture and stir (P & K). Then add the nuts, baking powder and flour (P & K). Mix until all the ingredients are combined (K).

Pour the batter into the coffee can to within 2 to 3 inches of the rim (P). Put the baking sheet in the oven and set the coffee can in the middle of the sheet (P). Bake for 45 minutes to 1 hour or until top rises and turns brown and a butter knife inserted into the middle of the loaf comes out crumb-free (P).

Remove the coffee can from the oven and let it cool 5 minutes (P). If the bread has risen above the rim, use a sharp knife to cut off the excess (P). Turn the can over and place it on a serving plate. Use a can opener to remove the bottom of the coffee can (P & K). Gently slide the loaf out of the can. Lay the loaf on its side on the plate and use a sharp knife to cut the loaf into slices about 1 inch thick (P).

Before serving, spread out a blanket, open sleeping bag, or tablecloth in a large space like the living room floor. Put pillows around this pallet and place bread and oranges in the center of the blanket. Everyone finds a comfortable spot and you can share the Arabian nights stories from books or make up your own. We had so much fun with this idea over the years that we used it as a jumping off point for a birthday slumber party one year, using bed sheets and old material tacked to the ceiling and walls of our playroom to make a "tent" and making invitations in the shape of a magic lamp.

THE CURIOUS GEORGE BANANA MILKSHAKE

If you have curious little monkeys around your house who need
as much energy as they burn, this tasty drink is a fun way to get kids to drink
milk and to make sure they get some potassium on days when they turn their
noses up at fruits and vegetables.

You might even get them to hold still long enough to read one of H. A. Rey's
easy-to-follow, brightly illustrated Curious George books. George usually
learns a lesson in the course of the story, so they are a great way to bring up
subjects like telling the truth, following instructions,
or what to do if you get lost.

Here's a high energy recipe your family can monkey around with:

You'll Need:

3 bananas
6 to 8 scoops of vanilla ice cream
Approximately 1 quart of whole milk
½ teaspoon vanilla extract

Blender
Cutting board
Plastic knives for cutting
Drinking straws
Ice cream scoop
Measuring spoons

Before You Cook:

• Peel the bananas and throw away the peels (P & K).
• Cut the bananas into 2- to 3-inch pieces (K).

Let's Cook!

Put the pieces in the blender and mix on low speed, stopping occasionally to scrape sides of the blender (P). Add the ice cream, milk, and vanilla, and blend until you reach a relatively smooth consistency. Pour into glasses and serve with straws (K).

SAFETY TIP: Please make sure that the pieces of banana are broken down by the blender until the "chunks" are small enough not to get stuck in small throats.

WINNIE THE POOH'S FAVORITE SNACK WHEN VISITING RABBIT

It's true that you should never judge others solely on the size of their brains. This seems to be especially true of bears. One bear in particular. Winnie the Pooh is known for being "a bear of very little brain," but it's clear when you read about his adventures in The Hundred Acre Wood that Pooh is also a bear with a big heart who always tries to be helpful to his friends Piglet, Eeyore, Christopher Robin, and the others.

Of course, Pooh is also a bear with a very big appetite, and this has gotten him into trouble more than once, which poor Rabbit can vouch for. Once when Pooh visited Rabbit, he ate so much that he became stuck in Rabbit's doorway and it took ages to get him out!

Here's one version of Winnie the Pooh's favorite snack; just be sure you don't eat so much of it that you get stuck in someone's doorway!

Scones or biscuits

You'll Need:

1 package of biscuits or
3 cups flour
½ teaspoon baking soda
2 teaspoons cream of tartar
½ cup softened butter or margarine
1 teaspoon sugar
¼ cup evaporated milk
¼ cup water
1 egg, beaten
¼ cup raisins

Baking sheets
Ruler
Sharp knife for cutting
Clean, dry paint brush or pastry brush
Mixing bowl
Mixing spoon
Measuring cup
Measuring spoons
Small bowl
Whisk or fork

Before You Cook:

- If you are making biscuits, preheat oven according to package directions (P). If you are making scones, preheat oven to 400°.
- Break the egg into a small bowl and throw away the shell (P & K). Use the whisk or fork to lightly beat the egg. Set aside the egg and the pastry brush until you need them.

- Dust the cutting board lightly with some of the flour (P & K).

Let's Cook!

Prepare the biscuits according to the directions on the package.

If you are making scones, put the flour, baking soda, and cream of tar-tar together in the large mixing bowl (P & K). Then put small amounts of the measured butter in the flour mixture and use your fingers to mix them together until the mixture looks and feels crumbly (P & K). Pour the milk and water into the flour mixture (P). Add the raisins (K) and stir until you have a medium-soft dough (P & K). Place the dough on the floured board and use your hands to lightly press the dough into a rectangle about 8 x 10 inches. Use the ruler to cut the dough into triangles with bases about 3 inches long (P). You should be able to cut about 16 scones out of the dough.

Place the triangles on your baking sheet (P & K). Brush the top of each scone with a little of the beaten egg (P & K). Bake for 20 minutes or until the scones are golden brown. Remove the baking sheet from the oven and use the spatula to put the scones on the plates you will serve.

Serve them warm, the way Winnie the Pooh likes them, with honey on the plate to dip them in accompanied by a big glass of milk to wash them down.

While you are snacking like Pooh, read some of the stories about Pooh and his friends in the books written by A. A. Milne. You'll find out how to play Pooh Sticks, a game that is still popular with children in England where Mr. Milne and his family lived. People often wonder where writers get their ideas for stories. In the case of the *Winnie the Pooh* stories, Mr. Milne modeled Christopher Robin on his small son, and the stories are actually tales about the stuffed animals that belonged to the little boy. Is there a favorite toy or doll at your house that you can make up adventures for?

Pecos Bill's Texas Trash

Pecos Bill was the greatest cowpuncher ever known on either side
of the Rockies. When he was a baby, he teethed on horseshoes and played with
grizzly bears instead of Teddy bears. When he grew up and had his own spread,
he met Slue-foot Sue, a cowgirl who was part coyote herself,
and they decided to get married.

On their wedding day, Slue-foot Sue wore a beautiful white dress
with a steel spring bustle under it. No sooner were they married than Sue
decided she had to ride Bill's horse, Widow Maker. Bill tried to warn her, but
Sue insisted, and sure enough, Widow Maker bucked her so hard she flew
around the new moon before she fell back to Earth. Her bustle was so springy
she bounced and flew around the moon again. As she fell back to Earth again,
Bill got out his lasso, but instead of bringing Sue back down to Earth,
she bounced so hard that she and Bill both flew around the moon
and were never seen again. Most people think they still live on the moon,
where they raised a bunch of kids just as wild and free as they are.

Most folks in West Texas say that when you hear it thundering, it's just the
children of Pecos Bill and Slue-foot Sue rough housing on the moon. The only
way Bill and Sue can get those kids settled down is to make them a batch of their
famous "Texas Trash." If you'd like to try it, here's their recipe:

You'll Need:

2 cups Rice Chex cereal
2 cups Cheerios
2 cups stick pretzels
1 cup salted, shelled peanuts
1 cup shelled pecans
2 teaspoons Worchestershire sauce
½ cup margarine or butter
½ teaspoon garlic salt

Large roasting pan
Big spoon
Serving bowl(s)
Paper towels

Before You Cook:

- Preheat the oven to 250°.
- Put butter, Worchestershire sauce, and garlic salt in a roasting pan (P & K). Place in the oven long enough to the melt butter, then remove.

Let's Cook!

Measure the remaining ingredients and pour them into the pan. Stir to mix and coat them with the butter mixture (P & K). Place the pan in the oven for 1 hour. Every 15 minutes, remove the pan, stir and turn the ingredients, then put pan back in the oven (P & K).

After 1 hour, remove the pan from the oven. Put a paper towel in a serving bowl and pour the Texas Trash into a bowl.

While munching Texas Trash, read some tall tales or trickster stories. In Native American stories, Coyote is the trickster. In African legends, the trickster is Ananzi, the spider. Try making up your own tall tales about natural events like what makes the thunder and lightning, why there is salt in the sea, or why volcanoes erupt.

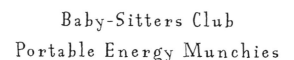

Baby-Sitters Club
Portable Energy Munchies

The Baby-Sitters Club books have become one of the most popular
preteen series in America. Girls love them because they deal with friendships,
resolving conflicts between friends, different kinds of family groups, siblings,
boys, and school. Parents love them because they show a group of kids
(girls and boys) who are positive, productive, and involved
in their families and communities.

Anyone familiar with the Baby-Sitters Club realizes that girls like Claudia,
Dawn, Mallory, and Stacey need a lot of energy to get through a day of school,
baby-sitting, and planning events like their Father-Daughter Picnic. They need
a high-energy, portable snack. Here's a terrific snack for the
preteens and teens at your house:

You'll Need:

1 box mini-pretzels
1 bag dried apricots
1 8-ounce box raisins
1 6-ounce bag semi-sweet chocolate morsels
3 cups Corn Chex cereal
2 cups Cheerios
1 cup shelled, salted peanuts

Plastic, resealable bags (sandwich or quart size)
Mixing bowl
Spoons for loading bags

Let's Cook!

Pour all of the above ingredients into mixing bowl. Mix together thoroughly with spoons and clean hands (K). Have one person hold a sandwich bag open over the mixing bowl while the other "shovels" ingredients into the bag (P & K). Seal and store to use for school snacks, hiking, after school snacks, or TV watching munchies.

Read one of the Baby-Sitters Club books and let it inspire you to plan an event in your own neighborhood: build a puppet theater out of cardboard boxes and scraps of materials around the house, then make your own hand puppets with papier maché heads and give puppet shows for younger neighborhood kids or at your local library or preschool; organize a sandlot pee-wee baseball game or soccer match in your neighborhood to teach little kids how to play. Preteens and teens: if you think adults will only say "no" to ideas you and your friends come up with to benefit people in your community, it just means you haven't asked the right adult yet. Keep trying!

THE LITTLE MERMAID'S DANISH DANISH

A lot of people who know me (both grown-ups and kids) meet my family and
assume that one of my favorite fairy tales must be Hans Christian Andersen's
The Little Mermaid.

On behalf of my daughter, let me set the record straight:
yes, I like a lot of Danish storyteller Andersen's tales; yes, I was especially fond
of the Danny Kaye musical about Hans Christian Andersen when I was a kid
(I have actually been known to hum "Wonderful Copenhagen" when I'm
dusting); and yes, my youngest daughter's name is Ariel.

But—

My favorite story by Andersen has always been "The Emperor's New Clothes."
I had a terrible crush on Danny Kaye and also hum songs from his other films
occasionally, and my daughter's name has more to do with Shakespeare than
animation or Andersen, but that, as they say, is a different story...

I should warn parents that, like the Brothers Grimm versions of familiar
fairy tales, Andersen's wonderful yarns are sometimes gruesome by modern
American standards, so I suggest parents read them through first, then share
them if they think it's appropriate for their children's age and understanding. I
once improvised the ending of "The Red Shoes" because I had completely forgot-
ten how grisly the ending was until I started reading it aloud to my two oldest
daughters, who were about 2 and 3 years old at the time.

Of course in my version, the girl learns her lesson and the red shoes
get tired, so she is able to take them off.

While you're deciding about the stories, try the Little Mermaid's favorite
Danish pastry. This recipe takes a while to prepare, so it's perfect for baking on
a cold night or a long, rainy afternoon, especially when you use the time that the
dough "rests" to make up an add-on story with one person starting the story,
reaching an exciting peak, then passing the next part of the story
to another person.

You'll Need:

2 packages dry yeast

¼ cup sugar

1 cup milk

4 cups all-purpose flour

3 eggs, separated

1 teaspoon salt

1 cup butter or margarine

Slivered almonds (optional)

Favorite marmalade or jam for filling

Oil

Fork

Butter knife

Sharp knife

Large bowl for mixing

3 Small bowls

Small saucepan

Mixing spoon

Measuring spoons

Measuring cup

Rolling pin

Cutting board for rolling out dough

Dish towel or small clean cloth large
enough to cover mixing bowl

Pastry brush or clean, medium-width
paint brush

Clock, watch or kitchen timer

Baking sheet

Spatula

Serving platter or plate

Before You Cook:

• Separate 2 eggs using two small bowls (for directions on how to separate, see Sleeping Beauty's 16th Birthday Cake) (P & K). Set aside.

• Preheat the oven to 400°.

Let's Cook!

Warm the milk slightly, about body temperature in a small saucepan over low heat. Do not scald the milk or make it too hot, as this will kill the yeast (P & K).

In a small bowl, combine the yeast with 1 tablespoon of sugar and 2 tablespoons of milk. Stir to dissolve the yeast and sugar gently (P & K). Set this mixture aside to "proof" for 10 minutes.

In the large mixing bowl, combine the flour, all but 2 tablespoons of the sugar, the remaining milk, 2 egg yolks (the yellow part you have separated), the salt, and, when it is through resting, the yeast mixture (P & K). Stir only enough to make the dry ingredients moist.

Flour your hands lightly (P & K) and mix the dough until the ingredients are thoroughly combined and form a smooth, springy dough that doesn't stick to your hands (P & K). Cover the bowl and put it in a warm, draft-less place (K). Let the dough rise for 15 minutes.

While the dough rises, flour the cutting board and rolling pin lightly (P & K). Have the butter ready for the next step.

When the dough has risen, turn it out on the floured cutting board (P & K). If the dough is very sticky, sprinkle it very lightly with a little extra flour (P & K) and re-flour the rolling pin (P & K). Roll the dough out on the cutting board (P & K) until it is about ½ inch thick. Use a butter knife to dot the dough with butter (not too much—about 2 to 3 tablespoons) (P & K). Lightly score the dough lengthwise into thirds (do not cut all the way through; these are just guidelines for the next step) (P). Fold the third on your right over the third in the middle (P & K). Now fold the third on the left over what was the third in the middle (P & K).

Turn the dough one quarter turn on the board and roll it out again, making it ½-inch thick (P & K). Dot the surface with butter as described above (P & K). Score it into thirds (P), and repeat the folding process (P & K).

Turn the dough to the left one quarter turn. Repeat the roll, dot, fold process until all of the butter has been used (P & K). Let the dough rest about 10 minutes.

While the dough is resting, use the oil to grease your baking sheet (P & K).

After it has rested, roll the dough out to about ½-inch thickness (P & K) in a rough rectangle. Score it lightly in thirds lengthwise (P). Put your marmalade or filling in a long, straight row on the third nearest to you (P & K), trying to keep it at least 1 inch away from the leading edge nearest you. Beginning at the edge near you, roll the dough over the filling and keep rolling it until you reach the "top" edge, the side farthest from you (P & K). About ½-inch from the other edge, dip your fingers in the water and lightly moisten the edge (P & K). Roll the dough all the way to the edge and apply light pressure to seal the edge (P & K). Use the sharp knife (P) to cut this roll into sections 1½- to 2-inches wide and lay these sections down flat on the greased baking sheet (K).

Separate the remaining egg (P & K). Combine the yolk in a small bowl with 1 tablespoon of milk, mixing well with the fork (P & K). Use the pastry brush to coat the top of each section with the egg mixture (P & K). Quickly sprinkle each piece with sugar (P &K) and almonds (K). Put the baking sheet in the oven and bake for 20 minutes (P).

When the pastries are browned, remove the sheet from the oven (P) and let cool slightly (no more than 5 minutes). Remove pastries from the sheet with the spatula and place them on serving plate (P & K).

Enjoy your Danish Danish while looking up Denmark on a map of the world or looking in a book on mythological creatures to find out about mermaids.

Sweets for The Sweetest

For the longest time growing up, I believed that "cooking" fell into two categories: one, stuff that is good for you (broccoli and chicken and dumplings are in this group), and two, stuff kids actually like to eat (this group being constructed almost entirely out of sugar).

I suppose kids wouldn't consider this any kind of a cookbook if it didn't include sweets. From the parents' perspective, you'll notice I included them at the end of the book, after the nutritious stuff.

One thing that our family has done to reduce the amount of time consumed in the cooking or baking process is to develop a basic cake recipe, a basic pie crust recipe and a cookie recipe everyone likes, then using them with different variations to create sweets for particular occasions. For example, a basic white cake recipe can be modified to become a chocolate birthday cake, the addition of coconut and a differently shaped cake pan makes it an Easter Bunny cake, and pouring it into lined muffin tins creates the ever-popular portable cake for school parties: cupcakes.

It took me about fifteen miserable years of soggy, tough, or underdone pie crusts to come up with a pie crust recipe that—I know you won't take my word for it—is just about foolproof. The great thing about it is that once you've mastered this one, you can use it for anything with a crust, including non-kid food like quiche.

I've used mainly fairy tale heroines for these sweets because that's how we think of them; something sweet and pretty that makes people smile, but of course, we couldn't leave out the sweetest person of all, that big, jolly guy in the red suit.

SLEEPING BEAUTY'S 16TH BIRTHDAY CAKE

The Princess Aurora had an odd sixteenth birthday party; because an evil fairy had put a curse on her when she was a baby, her party was kept very quiet and no spinning wheels were invited. But even with these precautions, she still pricked her finger on the spindle of a spinning wheel and fell asleep for a hundred years. And you thought you had to take long naps!

Most people think that Prince Charming awoke Princess Aurora, the Sleeping Beauty, with true love's first kiss. Actually, he woke her up by waving a slice of her 16th birthday cake under her nose and it smelled so wonderful she woke up so she could have a bit. Needless to say, they picked up the party where they had left off and they all lived happily ever after.

If you have a special occasion or a birthday coming up, this is a very festive cake. It doesn't necessarily have to be your sixteenth birthday. It's a great basic white cake recipe and you can change it to suit your own tastes or any occasion. For example, if you substitute blueberries for the strawberries, it becomes a perfect cake for Smurfs. For Father's Day, you can decorate it with milk chocolate frosting and pecan halves, and to perk up a blah week, use yellow food coloring and thin black licorice to turn it into a happy face.

You'll Need:

2½ cups flour

1¼ cups sugar

4 teaspoons baking powder

1 teaspoon salt

½ cup butter or margarine

1 cup milk

1 teaspoon vanilla extract

4 eggs

Red food coloring

1 to 2 pints fresh strawberries

Oil

1 can of vanilla frosting

3 mixing bowls

Measuring cup

Measuring spoons

2 8-inch cake pans

Waxed paper

Small bowl

Spoon for mixing

Whisk

Cutting board

Sharp knife

Knife for spreading

Wire racks for cooling

Before You Cook:

- Preheat the oven to 350°.
- Wash the strawberries and pull off the green leaves (P & K).

Let's Cook!

Cut enough strawberries into small pieces until you have 1 cup of them. Keep the rest of them whole and set aside. Use the oil to grease the cake pans. Line them with waxed paper. Then grease and lightly flour the inside of the waxed paper (P & K).

Separate the eggs; this means break them in half over the mixing bowl and let the clear part (the albumen) drip into the bowl and keep the yellow part (the yolk) in one half of the eggshell. Keep passing the yolk back and forth between the two eggshells until you've separated all of the clear part into the bowl (P & K). Put the yellow part into the small bowl, cover and refrigerate it to use in another recipe. Discard the egg shells and wash your hands before continuing.

Measure the flour, baking powder and salt into one bowl. In another bowl cream the sugar and butter together (P & K). Add the milk and the vanilla (P) and mix well (K). Pour about one-third of the flour mixture into the bowl with the other ingredients and mix until smooth (P & K). Add the next third of the flour and mix again. Repeat with the rest of the flour.

Use the whisk to stiffen the egg whites in the other bowl (P). Most people who fail at this simply give up too soon. This is a (P) job, but it goes much faster if the kids help watch the clock and talk to you while you're working. The whole process takes about 4 minutes and once you start, *don't stop*. Tilt the bowl slightly, use the longest whisk with greatest number of wires you can find. Beat the whites at about 150 strokes per minute for the first 2 minutes, then pick up speed and whip them faster but with the lightest touch possible for the next 2 minutes. You want the eggs to peak and to be stiff but not dry. Don't stop during the process. Make sure the whisk doesn't have any grease or oils on it when you start and there mustn't be any yellow from the egg in the whites. Sorry, but forks, spoons, and electric mixers won't work for this one.

When the whites have been beaten stiff, add them slowly to the other mixture (always add lighter ingredients to heavier ingredients, not the other way around) (P). Fold them into the batter with a wide, spreading spatula, literally folding the batter over the egg whites. Work them lightly and as little as possible to combine them. Gently stir in ¾ cup of strawberries and 3 to 4 drops of red food coloring (P & K). Pour batter into two cake pans and place pans in the oven and bake at 350° for 25 minutes or until a toothpick inserted in the middle of each pan comes out clean.

While the cake is baking, wash and dry thoroughly one of the mixing bowls (P & K). Open the frosting and put it in the bowl (P & K). Add the other ¼ cup of cut strawberries and enough food coloring, one drop at a time until you reach the pink color you like (P & K).

When the cake is done, remove it from the oven, let it cool slightly, then place a wire rack on top of each cake pan and turn it upside down (P). Carefully remove cake pan and paper from the cake and let cool completely.

When the layers are cool, turn one onto a cake plate and frost it (P & K). Then stack the next layer on top and frost it. On the top of the frosted cake, put 8 to 10 whole strawberries around the outside edge, like numbers on a clock face. Put one strawberry in the middle (P & K). Use a knife to lightly score the top from the middle strawberry out to the edges in wedge shapes for serving portions (P).

If it's someone's birthday, top the cake with candles. If not, enjoy dessert while someone reads *The Sleeping Beauty*.

CINDERELLA'S PUMPKIN PIE

Anyone who knows me understands that I am a big believer in recycling.
At our house, we turn coffee grounds, egg shells, vegetable tops, and peels
from potatoes and bananas into compost for our garden.
We also recycle papers, plastics, and glass.
So it always made sense to me that someone who did as much housework as
Cinderella would certainly be into recycling, too. You don't really believe that
after her beautiful coach was changed back into a pumpkin that someone as frugal as Cinderella would leave a perfectly good, if slightly used, pumpkin sitting
by the side of the road, do you?
Here, then, is what became of her pumpkin-coach and if you're running low
on friendly mice, you can always substitute children as helpers.

For Simple Pie Crust, You'll Need:

1 cup flour

½ teaspoon salt

⅓ cup shortening or cold, unsalted butter

Approximately 2 tablespoons water

Enough flour to dust a cutting board and a rolling pin

Mixing bowl

Measuring cup

Measuring spoons

Pastry cutter

Fork

Cutting board

Rolling pin

9-inch pie pan

Knife for cutting dough

Before You Cook:

• Preheat the oven to 425°.

Let's Cook!

Measure flour and salt into the mixing bowl (P & K). Add shortening and use the pastry cutter to combine those ingredients until they are all mixed well and about the size of peas (P & K). Add 1 tablespoon of water and mix with fork (P & K). Add another tablespoon of water and keep working dough lightly with the fork. Use more water, if necessary, about 1 tsp. at a time, until the dough can be pressed together in a ball. Cover the bowl and refrigerate the dough for 30 minutes to an hour.

After chilling the dough, dust the cutting board and rolling pin with
flour. Put the ball of dough in the center of the board and roll out with the
rolling pin (P & K). Turn the dough on the board about one-fourth turn
and roll again. Keep turning and rolling until the dough is round and slightly larger than the pie pan.

Fold the dough in half and in half again (P & K). *Do not press the dough
down or together when you fold it.* Lift the folded crust into the pie pan and gently unfold it until it covers the pie pan (P). Lightly press down the crust
into the bottom of the pie pan and against the sides of the pie pan (P & K).
Use the knife to trim off the excess crust, so that it is flush with the outside
rim of the pie pan. Prick the bottom of the crust with the fork 5 or 6 times
in random places on the bottom of the crust (K). Decorate the rim of the
pie crust by pressing down all the way around the crust with your fingers,
the handle of the fork, or any kitchen implement that makes a uniform
impression in the dough (P & K). Set the crust aside. Prepare the filling.

For Pumpkin Pie Filling, You'll Need:

1 6-ounce can solid pack pumpkin

2 eggs

¾ cup granulated sugar

¼ cup firmly packed brown sugar

½ teaspoon cinnamon

½ teaspoon ground ginger

½ teaspoon ground cloves

½ teaspoon salt

1 12-ounce can evaporated milk

1 tub whipped topping

Cinnamon

Mixing bowl

Whisk, fork or egg beater

Measuring spoons

Mixing spoons

Knife for testing

Before You Cook:

• Make sure the oven is still heated to 425°.

Let's Cook!

Break both eggs into the mixing bowl and discard shells (P & K). Use the whisk, fork, or egg beater to lightly beat the eggs (P & K). Add the pumpkin, sugars, seasonings, and evaporated milk and blend (P & K). Pour the filling into the pie crust. Put the pie into the oven and bake at 425° for 15 minutes. Lower the heat to 350° and continue to bake for 45 minutes, or until a knife inserted into the middle of the pie comes out clean (P & K).

Remove the pie from the oven and let it cool (P). Refrigerate the pie until you are ready to serve it. Use a knife to cut it into wedges. Top each slice with a generous dollop of whipped topping (P & K). If you like cinnamon, dust the topping with a tiny amount of cinnamon. If you prefer your pumpkin pie warm, you may serve the pie still warm and add a scoop vanilla ice cream to the top instead of the whipped topping.

Almost every country and culture has its own variation of the Cinderella story. Did you know in the French version, Cinderella's glass slipper wasn't glass, but made of fur? For fun, read *Cinderella*, then try to find the Italian version at the library. Or try making up your own modern version of the story.

THE QUEEN OF HEARTS' TARTS

Among so many sweet things one is bound to find one thing that is a bit tart.
When it comes to fairy tale royalty, the tartest of the tart has got to be Her
Majesty, the Queen of Hearts from *Alice's Adventures in Wonderland.* Not just
any member of the ruling class can get away with bashing hedgehogs around a
croquet ground and screaming, "Off with her head!"

But even the sourest puss of all has to have something sweet about her,
and the Queen's Tarts follow the same rule. Like this manic monarch herself, her
tarts are quite rich, and just as Alice discovered that nothing in Wonderland is
quite what it seems, you'll find that this elegant little dessert is
much more simple to make than it looks.

We're big Alice fans. Our children were shocked and amazed one day when
my husband and I burst into a spontaneous recitation of *The Jabberwock.* My
eldest daughters love to hear *The Walrus and the Carpenter,* and the youngest
one keeps examining new foods for labels reading, "Eat Me." One of my favorite
Wonderland customs is the Un-Birthday. These tarts are a great way to celebrate
anyone's next Un-Birthday at your house.

You'll Need:

One batch of Simple Pie Crust as described in Cinderella's Pumpkin Pie
and a small bag of dried beans

For the bottom layer:
2 eggs
½ cup sugar
1 package cream cheese
2 tablespoons sour cream
1 teaspoon vanilla extract

For the top layer:
4 cups fresh raspberries
2 tablespoons cornstarch
¼ cup water
⅔ cup sugar
½ cup raspberry jam
1½ tablespoons lemon juice
1 large chocolate bar

Mixing spoons
Fork
Cheese grater
Muffin pan
2 mixing bowls
Measuring cup
Measuring spoons
Whisk
Colander
Wire rack

Before You Cook:

- Preheat the oven to 450°.
- Prepare Simple Pie Crust. Use the oil to grease the sides and bottom of each opening in the muffin pan (K). Pull off small pieces of the pie crust dough and roll them out in rounds slightly larger than the muffin cups (P & K). Put the dough in the muffin pan, prick the bottom of each cup with the fork, and fill each cup about one-third full of dried beans (P & K).
- Place the muffin pan in the oven at 450° and bake for 15 minutes. Remove the pan from the oven, empty out the dried beans and set the tart shells aside (P). Lower the heat in the oven to 350°.

Let's Cook!

Break the eggs into the mixing bowl and discard the shells. Beat the eggs (P & K). Add the sugar, cream cheese, sour cream, and vanilla to the eggs and use the mixing spoon to beat until smooth (P & K). Fill each tart shell in the muffin pan just under half full of this mixture (P & K). Put the muffin pan in the oven and bake for 15 minutes while you prepare the next layer. Clean and pick over the raspberries and let them drain in the colander while you're working on the rest of the filling (P & K). Combine in a mixing bowl ¼ cup of water, 2 tablespoons of cornstarch, and ⅔ cup of sugar (P & K). Stir to dissolve the sugar and cornstarch and let it rest for 15 minutes (P & K). Add the jam, fresh berries, and 1½ tablespoons of lemon juice. Stir thoroughly until all ingredients are mixed well (P & K).

Raise the temperature of the oven to 375°. Remove the muffin pan from the oven and spoon the top layer over the cream cheese filling until each cup is filled just to the top of the muffin cup, but don't over-fill (P & K). Put the muffin pan back in the oven and bake for 10 minutes.

While this layer is baking, prepare the shaved chocolate. Using the side of the cheese grater for shredding, grate the chocolate bar, trying to get the most continuous chocolate curls that you can (P & K). Remove the muffin pan from the oven when the baking time is up (P). Carefully remove the tarts from the pan and let them cool on a wire rack. When completely cooled, garnish each tart with a little of the shaved chocolate (K). Refrigerate them until you are ready to serve them.

Now you have a delicious dessert to serve your family that is absolutely fit for a Queen!

Once you've tried the tarts with raspberries, talk about other berries or fruits you might like to try next time. Some people like them almost completely filled with the cream cheese layer, others don't care for the cream cheese at all and prefer them with only filling. By all means, use the recipe as the basic "pattern," then tailor them to your family's tastes.

SNOW WHITE'S EASY APPLE PIE

In the story of Snow White and the Seven Dwarfs, Show White's
evil stepmother, the vain queen, comes to the dwarfs' cottage dressed as an old
hag who offers Snow White a poisoned apple.

If you are an apple pie fan, you'll be happy to know that poison apple deaths were
down last year, and that there are so few evil, scheming queens around that it's
becoming increasingly easy to tell the good apples from the bad apples. Just to be
on the safe side, I do suggest getting the ingredients for this dessert from a
grocery store rather than from any peddler or old hag who might appear at your
kitchen door asking for a drink of water and offering you
suspicious apples in exchange.

Fairy tale dwarfs being fairy tale dwarfs, you'll understand when I tell you that
when they returned from their mine and discovered Snow White, they were
upset not only about their dear friend Snow White, but also
about the fact that they would not be getting any of her legendary apple pie.
Fortunately for all of us, the Prince discovered the beautiful Snow White in the
forest, gave her true love's kiss and revived her. He whisked her away to his cas-
tle where she could oversee the baking of apple pies
for the whole kingdom.

If everyone in your kingdom enjoys apple pie, try Snow White's
favorite recipe:

You'll Need:

1 9-inch pie crust, prepared from the Simple Pie Crust recipe for
Cinderella's Pumpkin Pie
4 cups apples (about 2 to 3 medium apples)
½ cup brown sugar
⅛ teaspoon salt
2 tablespoons cornstarch
¼ teaspoon cinnamon
⅛ teaspoon nutmeg
3 jars Dutch Apple Dessert baby food
1 small lemon
1 teaspoon vanilla extract
1 tablespoon butter or margarine

9-inch pie pan
Measuring cup
Measuring spoons
Peeler
Cutting board
Sharp knife
Mixing bowl
Mixing spoon

Before You Cook:

- Prepare the Simple Pie Crust and put it in the 9-inch pie pan. Do not bake it.
- Preheat the oven to 450°.
- Wash the apples and peel them (K). Core the apples (P).
- Wash the lemon, cut it in half, and set it aside.

Let's Cook!

Cut the apples into very thin slices (P) and put them into the mixing bowl. Add brown sugar, salt, cornstarch, cinnamon, nutmeg, baby food, 1 tablespoon of lemon juice, and vanilla. Stir until the ingredients are well combined and the apples are coated (P & K). Pour the apple mixture into the uncooked pie crust. Dot the top of the filling with the butter (P & K). Put the pie in the oven and bake at 450° for 20 minutes. Remove the pie from the oven and let it cool (P). Cut it into wedges and serve it topped with ice cream, cheese slices, or whipped topping.

PREPARATION TIP: We have found that the pie tastes best if you sneak bites of the apples and sing, "Hi ho, hi ho, it's off to work we go..." while doing the cooking. Originally, we had contests to see who could remember the names of all seven dwarfs. Now, the girls try to re-name the dwarves in as silly a vein as possible. For example, last round, we came up with Pouty, Flashy, Giggly, Scary, Perky, Hairy, and Bob.

IF YOU GIVE A KID SOMETHING SWEET...

According to Laura Numeroff, if you give a mouse a cookie, he's probably going to want a glass of milk...and that's just the beginning! In all of Numeroff's books, the characters begin by having a snack together and then get distracted by things to do around the house, just about the way things happen around any house with children.

My own children have loved these darling, easy to read books, and often interrupt the stories so they can do the activities we read about, like coloring a picture of our family to put up on the front of the refrigerator or taking a bubble bath.

So whether you're giving a moose a muffin or giving a pig a pancake, you'll enjoy these recipes for sweet treats that make a good accompaniment for reading Numeroff's stories or doing other fun things around your house...

For Mouse's Butterscotch Sand Cookies, You'll Need:

1½ cups all-purpose flour
½ teaspoon baking soda
½ teaspoon salt
½ cup butter or margarine
¾ cup brown sugar
¾ cup sugar
½ teaspoon vanilla extract
1 egg
1 6-ounce package butterscotch morsels
½ teaspoon cinnamon

2 mixing bowls
Spoon for stirring
Measuring cup
Measuring spoons
Baking sheets
2 small spoons
Spatula
Wire rack for cooling

Before You Cook:

• Preheat the oven to 350°.

Let's Cook!

In one mixing bowl, combine flour, baking soda, and salt (P & K). In the other bowl cream the butter and sugars together (P & K). Add the egg, vanilla, and cinnamon to the butter mixture and stir thoroughly (P & K).

Pour the egg mixture gradually into the flour mixture and stir after each addition (P & K) so batter is smooth. Pour the butterscotch morsels into the batter and stir until all the morsels are evenly dispersed (P & K). Put the dough in the refrigerator to chill for about 30 minutes.

When the dough has chilled, use teaspoons to drop the dough onto the baking sheets (P & K), about 1½ to 2 inches apart because the cookies "spread out" as they bake.

Put the baking sheet in the oven and bake 9 to 12 minutes, until the cookies are a light golden brown (P).

Remove the cookies from the oven (P) and let the sheet cool for just a few minutes. Remove the cookies from the baking sheet with the spatula (P & K) and place them on the wire rack to cool completely.

Most of the mice I know are particularly fond of butterscotch, but if the mice at your house (or the children) are not really keen about butter-scotch, feel free to omit them or substitute your family's favorite morsels or M & M's.

For Moose Muffins with Your Mother's Homemade Jam, You'll Need:

1½ cups flour
4 teaspoons baking powder
1 teaspoon salt
2 tablespoons sugar
⅓ cup molasses
1½ cups quick-cooking rolled oats
2 eggs
¾ cup milk
3 tablespoons butter or margarine
1 small orange

2 mixing bowls
Measuring cup
Measuring spoons
Grater
Small bowl
Whisk
Fork
Muffin pan
Paper or foil muffin cups
Small saucepan
Large spoon or ladle

Before You Cook:

- Preheat the oven to 400°.
- Wash and dry the orange. Gently grate the peel of the orange until you have about 1 tablespoon (P & K) and set aside.
- Put the muffin cups in the muffin pan (K), or if you don't have paper muffin cups, use oil to lightly grease each section of the muffin pan (K). Break the eggs into the small bowl (P & K) and discard the shells. Use the whisk to lightly beat the eggs (P & K). Set aside.
- Put the butter in the saucepan (K) and melt the butter over a very low heat (P). Remove the pan from the heat and let the butter cool to just above room temperature.

Let's Cook!

In one mixing bowl combine flour, baking powder, salt, and rolled oats (P & K). In the other mixing bowl mix the eggs, milk, melted butter, molasses, and orange rind (P & K). Gradually pour the egg mixture into the flour mixture, mixing with the fork only until all the ingredients are thoroughly moistened (P & K). The batter will be slightly lumpy.

Use a large spoon or ladle to fill each muffin cup about two-thirds full (P & K).

Place muffin pan in the oven and bake at 400° for 20 to 25 minutes until the tops of the muffins have risen and turned a deep, golden brown. Muffins are ready when a toothpick inserted into the center of a muffin comes out without any moisture or crumbs clinging to it (P & K).

Remove the pan from the oven and immediately remove muffins from pan, placing them on the wire rack to cool (P).

For Your Mother's Homemade Jam, You'll Need:

½ pound strawberries
½ pound sugar
Water, if needed

Colander
Masher
Mixing bowl
Sharp knife
Wooden spoon
Large saucepan
Measuring cup
Cutting board
Clean, sterile container with airtight lid

Before You Cook:

- Wash and drain the strawberries (K). Cut off the tops of the berries and half or quarter (P). Discard the tops.
- Put the cut berries into the mixing bowl and use a potato masher to crush them (P & K).

Let's Cook!

Put the crushed strawberry pieces into the saucepan with a very small amount of water (under ¼ cup) just to get them started (P & K). Put the saucepan on the burner at a medium-high setting until the berry mixture reaches the boiling point (P).

Add the sugar to the saucepan and stir until the sugar is dissolved (P & K). Keep stirring the mixture often to keep it from burning or scorching on the bottom of the pan (P & K). Cooking time should be about 15 to 20 minutes. Jam is ready when the syrup has thickened.

If the color is too light for you, add a couple of drops of red food coloring just before the end of the cooking time and stir the mixture thoroughly (P & K). Remove the saucepan from the heat and let the jam cool slightly (P). Pour or spoon the jam into your container, cover it, and refrigerate the jam until you're ready to use it on your Moose Muffins.

The biggest secret to good muffins is mixing them with a fork until the dry ingredients are moistened but not beaten. There are supposed to be lumps and over-mixing will just make the muffins tough and nobody likes tough Moose Muffins.

If you are making jam, please be careful if the container you are using is glass (canning jars, for example) because the mixture will be hot and the glass will conduct the heat almost instantly, burning small, helpful hands. The same is true, obviously, of metal containers. Also, because the jam is homemade, there are no preservatives or chemicals to guard against spoilage, so use it quickly and don't plan on keeping it more than a day or two, even if you seal it tightly and refrigerate it continuously.

For Pig's French Dessert Pancakes, You'll Need:

4 eggs

1 cup flour

2 tablespoons sugar

1 cup evaporated milk

¼ cup water

2 tablespoons instant hot chocolate mix

1 tablespoon butter or margarine

Oil

Chocolate or vanilla ice cream

Chocolate syrup

Whipped cream (optional)

Mixing bowl

Whisk

Measuring cup

Spoon

Saucepan

Small, shallow crepe pan or skillet (6-inch)

Spatula

Plate for holding cooked crepes

Ice cream scoop

Waxed paper

Before You Cook:

• Have the cooling plate and waxed paper handy. Melt the butter in the saucepan on a very low heat **(P)**. Remove from the heat and let cool **(P)**.

Let's Cook!

In the mixing bowl, break the eggs and discard the shells (P & K). Use the whisk to beat the eggs until slightly frothy (P). Add flour, sugar, and hot chocolate mix, mixing lightly, then add milk and water and whisk again (P & K). Beat melted butter into the batter with the whisk (P & K). Then let the batter rest in the refrigerator for 1 hour.

When you're ready to make the crepes, pour some of the batter into a clean, dry measuring cup (P & K). Heat about 1 tablespoon of the oil in the pan on a medium heat (P). When heated, lift the pan off of the heat and use the measuring cup to pour enough batter to cover the bottom of the pan with a very thin layer of batter (P). Return the pan to a medium heat and cook until the edges are dry and slightly crisp. Use the spatula to lift the edges of the crepe (P) and gently turn the crepe over in the pan cooking the second side for less than 1 minute (P). Use the spatula to loosen the crepe from the pan then slide it onto the cooling plate (P). While the next crepe is cooking, tear off a piece of waxed paper and place it over the first crepe (K). Repeat these steps until all of the batter is used (P), separating each crepe with waxed paper (K). Let the crepes cool.

When the crepes are cooled, place one on a dessert plate (K) and put a scoop of ice cream near the center of the crepe (P) using the scoop to slightly flatten the ice cream. Fold the edge of the crepe nearest to you toward the center and roll up the ice cream inside the crepe (P & K). Make sure the upper edge of the crepe ends up under the bulk of the crepe to hold it closed.

If you like, put a small dollop of whipped cream at one end of the crepe (K). Drizzle the chocolate syrup lightly over the crepe. Repeat until everyone has been served two crepes (P & K).

SANTA CLAUS'S FAVORITE
CHOCOLATE CHIP COOKIES

On Christmas Eve, after all the presents are wrapped, the tree is trimmed, the carols have been sung and we've cuddled up to read *The Night Before Christmas*, the very last thing to do before we snuggle into our beds to try to sleep so Christmas morning will come sooner is to put out a plate of snacks and goodies for Santa and his reindeer. Delivering gifts to everyone in the whole world in one night is hard work, so we always leave something good to eat for him and a note telling him thanks for stopping by. We have learned over the years that the reindeer are particularly fond of carrots, apples, and uncooked oats, while Rudolph, like Santa himself, has quite a sweet tooth.

You know that Santa is busy making and delivering toys at Christmas, but did you ever wonder what he gets up to the rest of the year? Most people are surprised to hear that Santa likes to work in his garden, swims and plays golf a lot in the summer, and actually makes a mean pot of chili when he's tinkering around in the kitchen. Santa laughs and says that one of his jobs around the house is to be a guinea pig for Mrs. Claus when she's trying out new recipes. The Clauses like to putter around the kitchen together and they have their favorite recipes just as the rest of us do.

So, if you want to make Santa a treat this Christmas Eve (and have a few left over to munch on yourself), why not try this recipe straight from the Claus kitchen...

You'll Need:

1 cup butter or margarine
¾ cup brown sugar
½ cup granulated sugar
1 teaspoon vanilla extract
2 eggs
1 teaspoon baking soda
¼ teaspoon salt
¼ teaspoon cinnamon
1 cup uncooked instant oats
½ cup chopped walnuts
½ cup chopped pecans
1 12-ounce bag of semi-sweet chocolate morsels

Mixing bowl
Measuring cup
Measuring spoons
Spoon for stirring
Baking sheets
Small spoons for dropping dough
Wire rack
Spatula

Before You Cook:

- Preheat the oven to 350°.
- If you've bought whole walnuts and pecans, you'll need a sharp knife and a cutting board. Shell the nuts **(K)**, chop them into small pieces **(P)**, and set them aside.

Let's Cook!

In one mixing bowl, measure the flour, salt, and baking soda (P & K). In the other bowl, cream together the butter and sugars until smooth (P & K). Add vanilla, cinnamon, and eggs and beat the mixture until it is thoroughly blended. Add the flour mixture a little at a time and stir well for each addition (P & K). Pour oatmeal into the bowl and blend thoroughly. Add the nuts and chocolate morsels until they are well distributed throughout the mixture (P & K). Cover the bowl and put it in the refrigerator to chill for about 1 hour.

When the dough is chilled, remove from the fridge. Each person who is helping needs two small spoons. Scoop dough out of the bowl with one spoon and use the other spoon to scrape the dough off onto the baking sheet. Try to space the cookies at least 2 inches apart, as they spread out while baking (P & K). When the baking sheet is full, place it in the oven and bake for 9 to 12 minutes, until the cookies are a golden brown. Remove sheet from the oven and let it cool for just a few minutes. Use a spatula to remove the cookies from the baking sheet and place them on a wire rack to finish cooling (P). When cooled, stack some of the cookies on a plate and set out for Santa to enjoy.

If your family has questions about Santa and the North Pole, find a book called *Santa Claus Book*, by Alden Perkes. Do you know how Santa invented toys, or how he gets all those things in one bag, or how to make sure that Santa knows what you want for Christmas? You'll find the answers to these and many other questions in Mr. Perkes's book.

Afters....

The "afters" are the little something at the end of a long, sumptuous meal that puts the finishing touch on it. I hope after reading through this book you've discovered that the food you prepared together is wonderful, but the time together, building memories that will last through your life and possibly into the next generation, is the real feast.

I'll always remember my husband and our friend, Patrick, clanking and singing in the kitchen, preparing pound after pound of boiled shrimp for me when I was eight months pregnant and had a yen for seafood; I'll remember my eldest daughter "signing" the kitchen by painting her small hand with ketchup and making a perfect print on the wall; I'll remember the expression on my middle daughter's face the first time we gave her a segment of grapefruit to taste (I didn't know it was humanly possible to wrinkle up your entire body); I'll remember the sight of my youngest daughter standing on a chair next to her father at the cutting board learning with rapt attention the intricacies of how to make a pizza; I'll remember dancing the tango with my husband in the kitchen one Sunday while pancakes bubbled on the griddle and my daughters rolled their eyes and mumbled, "They're doing it again," between syrupy bites.

What will you remember?

Is the kitchen in your house the awful little space where you're forced to go and do dishes every day, or the room where the sights and sounds and smells are hundreds of memories in bottles, like spices, that can conjure up happy, important or funny times with the people most precious to you, past and present?

Make dinner together tonight. Ask how school was. Tell them what your mom cooked for you when you needed a lift. Try to guess each other's favorite foods.

No matter how large or how small your family is, cooking together can be the most important few minutes of your life. And remember—the most important ingredient in any dish is always love.

Index